The Catholic Choirbook

Anthology I

ANTHOLOGY I IS A COMPANION VOLUME TO
THE CATHOLIC CHOIRBOOK CHOIR TRAINING GUIDE

MW01293464

The Catholic Choirbook Anthology
I

Editors
Ellen Doll Jones, CAGO
Noel Jones, AAGO

Thanks to Kevin Allen for permission to include his compositionTantum Ergo,
featured under the opening credits on the
2009 Church Music Association of America Colloquium Video.
www.kevinallen.info

and to

Matthew Curtis
for Choral Training and Sample Audio/Videos.
www.choraltracks.com

This book available in Hardcover

Frog Music Press

201County Road 432 • Englewood, TN 37329
noeljones@usit.net
www.frogmusic.com

www.thecatholicchoirbook.com

This choirbook is created under the protection of Creative Commons 3.0,
which permits freely copying and sharing of the contents of this book
but does not permit the publishing of Creative Commons music
and text from this book for commercial purpose without permission.

The Catholic Choirbook Series

In Print & For Download

The Catholic Choirbook I
General

The Catholic Choirbook II
Tantum ergo

The Catholic Choirbook III
Cantate Domino

The Catholic Choirbook IV
Locus Iste

The Catholic Choirbook V
Gratia Plena

The Catholic Choirbook Anthology I
Music from the Choirbook Series
Soft Cover • ISBN 1461103630
Hardbound Dark Blue Library Cloth
Hardbound Full Color Laminate Cover

The Catholic Choirbook Choir Training Guide
A Companion Director's Guide to using The Anthology I

www.TheCatholicChoirbook.com

The Catholic Choirbook Series contains music suitable for choirs of the Catholic church, with texts in both Latin and English. The rich heritage of Catholic music has continued unbroken for centuries in churches and cathedrals that understand the need for music which is appropriate in both style and text for the Catholic Mass.

The series is more than just a collection of choir music. Rather, it is based upon the need for music - of varying difficulties, for varied sizes of groups, and of value as teaching material to improve the abilities of the singers.

How large does a choir need to be to sing this music? Some of the largest works call for SSAATTBB to create the lush harmonies. They may be sung by 40 singers or by 8 singers. But what if you have only Sopranos, Altos and Tenors and no Bass singers? Play the Bass part on the organ, a cello or bassoon. If it's a loud, vigorous piece, use brass instruments to fill out the missing voices. Composers wrote, and still write, for the singers they have available. Compromise is always a possibility.

Modern editors lavish the music with slurs, showing the singer exactly what notes are sung to each vowel. This is a recent practice, since in early music it was understood that every note after a vowel is sung to that vowel, until a new vowel appears. This makes the music cleaner-appearing on the page and easier to follow. Need a slur as a reminder? Pencil it in. Later works that were composed with slurs, have them in place.

In the back of the book you will find a few Gregorian chants which have connections to works of the same name in this collection. The Tantum Ergo by Palestrina uses much of the original chant melody in the soprano line, for example. Visit www.musicasacra.com to purchase or download The Parish Book of Chant, from which these chants have been taken, to learn more about them. There are really not that many words to learn to sing in Latin. It's a lot easier than English because the vowel sounds are always the same - none of this "read" and "red" business we suffer through in English. So once you can sing a few pieces in Latin, it all begins to get easy. To help you and your choir, you may have noticed that we try to put more than one musical setting of a Latin text in our choir books. Perfecting a choir's abilities by singing various versions of Adoramus Te, for example, and getting their diction clean and precise, will spill over into other works they sing.

Many of these Anthems (words in English) and Motets (words in Latin) are linked on our web site to Matthew Curtis's www.Choraltracks.com site. These are links to performances and practice files. It's a great way to get to know the music. If you subscribe to his site, you can access the training videos which enhance each individual part, but still enable you to hear all of the choral parts together. It's a great help to a choir to be able to listen to the music, as well as their individual parts, outside of choir rehearsal. Singers absorb much more information about how to sing a piece by listening to it than they realize

Many choir directors have little or no opportunity to get out, hear other choirs, and gain experience that could help them learn how to improve and build a choir. This Anthology is backed up by lessons which are available on our web site. They feature music from The Anthology and how it can be used to train your choir, as well as provide music for the liturgy. Hymns both old and new appear in this book that may be sung as solos, or by the choir when singing a full anthem may not be possible. And to make it even more useful to you, bulletin notes will be available to insert in your church bulletin about the music you are singing. The Anthology is a book of music, music that can become part of the life of your church.

www.thecatholicchoirbook.com

www.musicasacra.com

www.kevinallen.info

www.choraltracks.com

and our sister sites:

www.basicchant.com

www.thecatholichymnal.com

Thomas Holbeck
4. Voc.
ALTVS.
W. Byrd.
Yrie elei- son ij. Kyri-
e eley- son.
Hriste elei- son, ij.
Christe elei- son.
Yrie eleison. ij. ij. Kyrie e- lei-son,
ij. Kyri- e elei- son,
T in terra pax, hominibus bonæ volunta-
tis, benedicimus te, glori-ficamus te, ij.
ij. Gratias agimus tibi, propter magnam gloriam
¶.j.

Ave Regina Coelorum	Guillaume Dufay	ATB
Kyrie	William Byrd	ATB
Gloria	William Byrd	ATB
Credo	William Byrd	ATB
Sanctus	William Byrd	ATB
Agnus Dei	William Byrd	ATB
Stabat Mater	Giovanni Battista Pergolesi	Continuo/SA
Jesu! Rex Admirabilis	Giovanni Pierluigi da Palestrina	SAB
Non Nobis Domine	Tune of Philip Van Wilder	SAB
O Bone Jesu	Michelangelo Grancini	SAB
Adoramus Te Christe	Giovanni Pierluigi da Palestrina	SATB
Adoramus Te Christe	Francesco Gasparini	SATB
Adoramus Te Christe	Giovanni Pierluigi da Palestrina	SATB
Adoramus Te Christe	Theodore Dubois	SATB
Alleluia Al Vangelo	Andrea Gabrieli	SATB
Almighty And Everlasting God	Orlando Gibbons	SATB
Angelus Autem Domino	Felice Anerio	SATB
Assumpta Est	Peter Phillips	SATB
Ave Maria	Jacob Arcadelt	SATB
Ave Maria	William Byrd	SATB
Ave Maria	Giacomo Fogliano	SATB
Ave Maria	Francisco Guerrero	SATB
Ave Verum	Edward Elgar	Organ/SATB
Ave Verum	William Byrd	SATB
Ave Verum	Wolfgang Amadeus Mozart	Organ/SATB
Cantate Domino	Giuseppi Pitoni	SATB
Cantate Domino	Hans Leo Hassler	SATB
Cantate Domino	Giovanni Croce	SATB
Cantate Domino	Wolfgang Amadeus Mozart	SATB
Crux Fidelis	King John IV of Portugal	SATB
God So Loved The World	John Goss	SATB
God So Loved The World	John Stainer	SATB
Hide Not Thou Thy Face	Richard Farrant	SATB
If Ye Love Me	Thomas Tallis	SATB
Jesu Dulcis Memoria	Tomás Luis de Victoria	SATB
Locus Iste	Anton Bruckner	SATB
Lord, For Thy Tender Mercy's Sake	Richard Farrant	SATB
Miserere Mei	Tomás Luis de Victoria	SATB
O Bone Jesu	Marc'Antonio Ingegniere	SATB
O Magnum Mysterium	Pedro de Cristo	SATB
O Magnum Mysterium	Tomás Luis de Victoria	SATB
O Sacrum Convivium	R. Remondi	SATB
O Sacrum Convivium	Edward D'Evry	SATB
Panis Angelicus	Louis Lambillotte	Organ/SATB
Prayer Of King Henry IV	Henry G. Ley	SATB
Remember, Remember Not	Henry Purcell	SATB
Tantum Ergo	Giovanni Pierluigi da Palestrina	SATB
Tantum Ergo	Déodat de Sévrác	SATB
Tantum Ergo	Kevin Allen	SATB
Thou Knowest Lord	Henry Purcell	SATB
Cantate Domino	Giovanni Andrea Cima	SATB Continuo
Domine Deus	Antonio Lucio Vivaldi	A/SATB Continuo
Ave Maria	Robert Parsons	SATTB
Ave Maria	Anton Bruckner	SATTB
Adoramus Te Christe	Orlando di Lasso	SSA
Cantate Domino	Daniel Friderici	SSA
Salve Regina	Sigismund Ritter von Neukomm	SSA
Crucifixus	Antonio Lotti	SSAATTBB
Hear My Prayer, O Lord	Henry Purcell	SSAATTBB
Miserere Mei	Antonio Lotti	SSAATTBB
Beati Quorum Via	Charles Villiers Stanford	SSATTB
Adoramus Te Christe	William Byrd	Unison/Continuo

The Catholic Choirbook
Choir Training Guide

The Catholic Choirbook Series started out as a set of books of music suitable for the Catholic liturgies. The goal was to make them large, easy to read, and yet light in weight, limiting them to under 130 pages each.

But a recurrent thought was the need for one book with material that was affordable - which meant increasing the number of pages, the inexpensive part of publishing - and music that is hand-picked to make it useful not just for singing at Mass, but also as a tool for the director to use in training a choir.

But merely handing a book of music to a director and saying, "Get on with it!", assumes that the director knows how to take a choir beyond just learning notes and singing. There are many directors out there who have not had the opportunity to receive training as a choral director.

Today, with the internet, it is possible to study using both audio and video.

On our website, www.thecatholicchoirbook.com, The Anthology page lists the music in the book in the order of lessons, to assist you, the director, in building your choir to a higher level of musical ability.

It would be ideal if each choir member could have a bound copy of The Anthology in hand during rehearsals. Bound in paperback it will last quite awhile and the optional hard-bound copies even longer. But this assumes a music budget, if there is one, that could afford that. Since many parishes have no money for music, you will be able to print the matching pages from The Catholic Choirbook Series for your choir and the lessons as well for free as they are posted.

The lessons will be printed and bound, and available for purchase as each section is completed, for your convenience. Audio and video files will be available to supplement the lessons, some for free download, but also for purchase in CD and DVD format for your library.

Bulletin notes about the music studied will be available for your church bulletin.

An email list announces the posting of lessons and materials. You will need to sign up for that list, for which there is no charge. Visit www.thecatholicchoirbook.com to join.

Thank you for sharing with me the goal of improving music throughout the Catholic Church. Your generous donations and purchases assist us in carrying on this work.

Noel Jones, AAGO

Composers

Tantum Ergo	*Kevin Allen*
Angelus Autem Domino	*Felice Anerio*
Ave Maria	*Jacob Arcadelt*
Ave Maria	*Anton Bruckner*
Locus Iste	*Anton Bruckner*
Ave Maria	*William Byrd*
Ave Verum Corpus	*William Byrd*
Kyrie	*William Byrd*
Gloria	*William Byrd*
Credo	*William Byrd*
Sanctus	*William Byrd*
Agnus Dei	*William Byrd*
Adoramus Te Christe	*William Byrd*
Cantate Domino	*Giovanni Andrea Cima*
O Magnum Mysterium	*Pedro de Cristo*
Cantate Domino	*Giovanni Croce*
O Sacrum Convivium	*Edward D'Evry*
Adoramus Te Christe	*Theodore Dubois*
Ave Regina Coelorum	*Guillaume Dufay*
Ave Verum	*Edward Elgar*
Hide Not Thou Thy Face	*Richard Farrant*
Lord, For Thy Tender Mercy's Sake	*Richard Farrant*
Ave Maria	*Giacomo Fogliano*
Cantate Domino	*Daniel Friderici*
Alleluia Al Vangelo	*Andrea Gabrieli*
Immutemur Habitus	*José Mauricio Nunes Garcia*
Adoramus Te Christe	*Francesco Gasparini*
God So Loved The World	*John Goss*
O Bone Jesu	*Michelangelo Grancini*
Ave Maria	*Francisco Guerrero*
Cantate Domino	*Hans Leo Hassler*
O Bone Jesu	*Marc'Antonio Ingegniere*
Crux Fidelis	*King John IV of Portugal*
Panis Angelicus	*Louis Lambillotte*
Adoramus Te Christe	*Orlando di Lasso*
Prayer Of King Henry IV	*Henry G. Ley*
Crucifixus	*Antonio Lotti*
Miserere Mei	*Antonio Lotti*
Ubi Duo	*Claudio Monteverdi*
Ave Verum	*Wolfgang Amadeus Mozart*
Cantate Domino	*Wolfgang Amadeus Mozart*
Salve Regina	*Sigismund Ritter von Neukomm*
Adoramus Te Christe I	*Giovanni Pierluigi da Palestrina*
Adoramus Te Christe II	*Giovanni Pierluigi da Palestrina*
Jesu! Rex Admirabilis	*Giovanni Pierluigi da Palestrina*
Tantum Ergo	*Giovanni Pierluigi da Palestrina*
Ave Maria	*Robert Parsons*
Stabat Mater	*Giovanni Battista Pergolesi*
Cantate Domino	*Giuseppi Pitoni*
Hear My Prayer, O Lord	*Henry Purcell*
Remember, Remember Not	*Henry Purcell*
Thou Knowest Lord	*Henry Purcell*
O Sacrum Convivium	*R. Remondi*
Tantum Ergo	*Déodat de Sévrác*
Beati Quorum Via	*Charles Villiers Stanford*
God So Loved The World	*John Stainer*
If Ye Love Me	*Thomas Tallis*
Verily, Verily I say Unto You	*Thomas Tallis*
Jesu Dulcis Memoria	*Tomás Luis de Victoria*
Miserere Mei	*Tomás Luis de Victoria*
O Magnum Mysterium	*Tomás Luis de Victoria*
Vere Langoures Nostros	*Tomás Luis de Victoria*
Domine Deus	*Antonio Lucio Vivaldi*
Non Nobis Domine	*Philip Van Wilder*

FEAST OF CORPUS CHRISTI

William P. Mahrt, PhD, is a professor in the Department of Music at Stanford University, where he teaches Medieval and Renaissance music and directs the Stanford Early Music Singers. His scholarship deals with the relation of music and liturgy and music and poetry, as well as the music of Brahms. Dr. Mahrt was a founding member of the St. Ann Choir in 1963, and has been its director most years since 1964. He frequently leads workshops in the singing of Gregorian chant and the sacred music of the Renaissance and has lead many tours on music and liturgy to English cathedrals.

This article is from a booklet of translations of the choral works that the St. Ann Choir sings, created for the congregation to use to follow the singing of the texts. It explains, very concisely, much about music that you will find here in The Anthology. Some of these translations appear here, and we are grateful for their use.

To view the entire set of translations as well as read more about Dr. Mahrt and his choir:

http://www.stannchoir.org

INTRODUCTION: MOTETS

William P. Mahrt

Our sung Mass is based upon Gregorian chant, the fundamental music of the Roman liturgy. This liturgy is complete when sung only in chant, with people, choir, lectors, and priest chanting parts suitable to their different roles. The chants differ as their functions differ: for example, meditation chants which accompany the lessons are highly elaborate settings of their texts, while processional chants are somewhat more concise and project a greater sense of rhythmic motion. The tradition of chant is so extensive that there is a normative set of pieces for almost any occasion. In the course of a year, the choir sings well over three hundred pieces for the Proper of the Mass, while the congregation sings over thirty different melodies for the Ordinary.

Yet the chant basis can be amplified by the interpolation of polyphony (music for more than one part), whether for organ or choir. Polyphonic music serves a different function in the liturgy: the complexity of parts and the harmony of the whole convey to the listener a sense of cosmic order that is conducive to an interior order, to a meditation that is in harmony with the Creator and creation.

Although polyphonic music has a voluntary character—none is required by the liturgy—classical vocal polyphony and music for the pipe organ are explicitly mentioned as particularly desirable, as significant parts of the Church's "Treasury of Sacred Music." (Second Vatican Council, Constitution on the Sacred Liturgy, ¶112, 116, 120). The two major kinds of traditional vocal polyphony are the Mass and the motet. While we sing polyphonic Masses on the major feast days of the year, motets play a role in every liturgy, particularly as an enhancement of the offertory and communion. Since they are chosen voluntarily, different motets may be sung on any day from year to year, and so they are not included in the normal programs for Mass. Rather, the texts of our motets are presented in this booklet so that the congregation may follow them with translations, whatever motet we may choose. The numbers of the motets are indicated on the board at the front of the church.

"Motet" comes from the French mot, "word," since a motet is a piece based upon an added text. In the Middle Ages, this meant literally that a tenor voice would sing a chant with its own text, while one or more upper parts would sing additional texts (as in #13, 91, and 194). But even with motets of the Renaissance—the period from which most of our motets come—there is still a sense that the motet is an added text: for example, after singing the proper communion antiphon, we choose to add another text and its musical setting, for the sake of enhancing meditation and reflection after the communion. These added texts are often drawn from the Psalms, the Church's canonical book of songs. But often the route by which they are adopted passes through liturgical use, many texts having been borrowed from the Divine Office—particularly responsories from Matins (e.g., #119-20) and antiphons to the Magnificat from Vespers (e.g., #103). Motets are also based upon favorite prayer texts, for example, Ave Maria (#23–30). Here the texts vary somewhat, since the second, non-scriptural part of the prayer was only beginning to be standardized in the Renaissance. Other motets stem from a tradition of devotional texts. A good example is O bone Jesu (#154-57), a series of brief acclamations, some drawn from scripture, whose compilation is traditionally ascribed to St. Bernard. Another way of amplifying upon a liturgical communion antiphon is simply to employ its proper Gregorian melody in a polyphonic piece. We sing a number of such settings of the communion antiphons by Heinrich Isaac from the collection Choralis Constantinus. They are included here for completeness, though, strictly speaking, they are not motets.

This collection represents motets the choir has sung over nearly forty years, some sung rather rarely, some favorites sung quite regularly. Among our favorites are Byrd, Ave verum; Josquin, Tu solus qui facis mirabilia and Tu pauperum refugium; La Rue, O salutaris Hostia; Palestrina, Sicut cervus; Purcell, Thou Knowest, Lord, the Secrets of our Hearts; Rore, Sicut cervus; and Victoria, Ave Maria; all motets used throughout the year. For the specific parts of the liturgical year: Tallis, Sancte Deus and Victoria, O vos omnes for the Passion; Lassus, Surrexit Pastor bonus for Easter; Gallus, Factus est repente for Pentecost; and Mouton, Cæleste beneficium for St. Ann.

We invite you to use this collection [of translations] as you find it helpful: the texts could form a suitable basis for prayer and meditation, and the motet texts for the day could easily be reviewed before Mass. We have tried to give quite literal English translations, so that those with at least a smattering of Latin may follow the Latin text, glancing at the English when needed. We have nonetheless tried to make the translations acceptable to be read in themselves, so that others may simply read the English either before or during the singing of the motet. Where the Latin text is from the scriptures, we have used Challoner's Douai-Rheims version, to be consistent with the texts of the Latin Vulgate Bible used in the liturgy. The texts are arranged in alphabetical order by title; an index of composers is supplied at the end, with a brief supplement for the second printing.

To see the entire collection of translations and learn more about Dr. Mahrt and the St. Ann Choir visit:

WWW.STANNCHOIR.ORG

te gloriosus apostolorum ch
te prophetarū laudabilis
te per orbem terrarum scta
te martirū candidatus lau
Te deum laudamus: te
te aeternū ptrem oīs terra
Vidi turbam magnam quam dinumerare nemo poterat, ex omnibus gentibus stantes ante thronum. (Apoc. VII, IX.)

ADORAMUS TE, CHRISTE

Antiphon for Good Friday Liturgy

We adore thee, O Christ, and we bless Thee,
because by Thy holy cross Thou hast redeemed the world.
O Lord, who suffered for us, have mercy on us.

Giovanni Pierluigi da Palestrina
c. 1525-1594

1
S
A
T
B
A - do - ra - mus te Chris - - - - te, et
5
be - ne - di - ci - mus ti - - - - bi, qui - a per sanc - tum cru - cem

copying & sharing of this music is permitted under creative commons 3.0 • the anthology I • www.thecatholicchoirbook.com

9
tu - am re - de - mis - ti - mun - - - dum. Qui pas - sus es pro
tu - am re - de - mis - ti - mun - - - dum. Qui pas - sus es pro
tu - am re - de - mis - ti - mun - - - dum. Qui pas - sus es pro
tu - am re - de - mis - ti - mun - - - dum. Qui pas - sus es pro
13
no - bis Do - mi - ne, Do - mi - ne mi - se - re no - bis.
no - bis Do - mi - ne, Do - mi - ne mi - se - re - re no - bis.
no - bis Do - mi - ne, Do - mi ne mi - se - re - re no - bis.
no - bis Do - mi - ne, Do - mi - ne mi - se - re - re no - bis.

 copying & sharing of this music is permitted under creative commons 3.0

ADORAMUS TE, CHRISTE

Antiphon for Good Friday Liturgy

We adore thee, O Christ, and we bless Thee,
because by Thy holy cross Thou hast redeemed the world.
O Lord, who suffered for us, have mercy on us.

Francesco Gasparini
1668-1727

copying & sharing of this music is permitted under creative commons 3.0 • the anthology I • www.thecatholicchoirbook.com

 copying & sharing of this music is permitted under creative commons 3.0

17
mun - dum, red - e - mi - sti mun - - - -
dum, red - e - mi - sti mun - - - - - - - - - -
e - mis - ti mun - - dum, red - e - mi - - sti mun - - - dum,
red - e - mis - ti mun - - - - - - - - - - - - - -
17
21
dum, red - e - mi - sti, red - e - mi - sti mun - - - - dum.
dum, red - - - - - e - mi - sti, mun - - - - - dum.
red - e - mi - sti, mun - - - - - - - - - - dum.
dum, red - e - mi - sti mun - - - - - - - dum,
21

ADORAMUS TE CHRISTE

Antiphon for Good Friday Liturgy
William Mahrt, Translation

We adore thee, O Christ,
and we bless thee:
because by thy holy cross
thou hast redeemed the world.

Orlando di Lasso
c1532-1594

 copying & sharing of this music is permitted under creative commons 3.0

copying & sharing of this music is permitted under creative commons 3.0 • the anthology I • www.thecatholicchoirbook.com

ADORAMUS TE CHRISTE

William Mahrt, Translation

We adore thee, O Christ,
and we bless thee:
because by thy holy cross
thou hast redeemed the world.

William Byrd
c.1540-1623

1
A - - - do - ra - mus te
5
Chri - - - - - ste, et be - ne - di - ci-mus ti -

 copying & sharing of this music is permitted under creative commons 3.0

bi:
Qui - a per san-ctam cru - - - - cem tu - am
re - de-mi-sti mun - dum, re - de-mi-sti
mun - - - - - - - dum, re-de - mi - sti mun - dum.

copying & sharing of this music is permitted under creative commons 3.0 • the anthology I • www.thecatholicchoirbook.com

ADORAMUS TE CHRISTE

Antiphon for Good Friday Liturgy
William Mahrt, Translation

We adore thee, O Christ,
and we bless thee:
because by thy holy cross
thou hast redeemed the world.

Giovanni Pierluigi da Palestrina
1525-1594

ECCE. PANIS. ANGELORUM

1
S
Ad - - - o - ra - mus te, Chris - - - - te,
A
Ad - - - o - ra - mus te, Chris - - - - te, et
T
Ad - - - o - ra - mus te, Chris - - - - te, et
B
Ad - - - o - ra - mus te, Chris - - - - te, et
1

 copying & sharing of this music is permitted under creative commons 3.0

copying & sharing of this music is permitted under creative commons 3.0 • the anthology I • www.thecatholicchoirbook.com

 copying & sharing of this music is permitted under creative commons 3.0

copying & sharing of this music is permitted under creative commons 3.0 • the anthology I • www.thecatholicchoirbook.com

ADORAMUS TE, CHRISTE

Antiphon for Good Friday
William Mahrt, Translation

We adore thee, O Christ,
and we bless thee:
because by thy holy cross
thou hast redeemed the world.

François-Clément Théodore Dubois
1837-1924

 copying & sharing of this music is permitted under creative commons 3.0

copying & sharing of this music is permitted under creative commons 3.0 • the anthology I • www.thecatholicchoirbook.com

19
p
et be-ne-di - ci-mus ti - bi.
A - do-ra-mus te, Chri - ste!
et be-ne-di - ci-mus ti - bi.
A - do-ra-mus te, Chri - ste!
et be-ne-di - ci - ti - bi.
A - do-ra-mus te, Chri - ste!
et be-ne-di - ci - ti - bi.
A - do-ra-mus te, Chri - ste!
19
mf
p

 copying & sharing of this music is permitted under creative commons 3.0

ALLELUIA AL VANGELO

Andrea Gabrieli
1510-1586

1
S
Al - le - lu - ia, al - - - - le - lu - ia, al - le - lu -
A
Al - le - lu - ia, al - le - - - - - lu - ia, al - le - lu -
T
Al - le - lu - ia, al - le - lu - ia, al - le - lu -
B
Al - le - lu -
1

copying & sharing of this music is permitted under creative commons 3.0 • the anthology I • www.thecatholicchoirbook.com

 copying & sharing of this music is permitted under creative commons 3.0

copying & sharing of this music is permitted under creative commons 3.0 • the anthology I • www.thecatholicchoirbook.com

ALMIGHTY AND EVERLASTING GOD

Collect, 3rd Sunday after Epiphany
1549 Book of Common Prayer

Almighty and everlasting God,
mercifully look upon our infirmities,
and in all our dangers and necessities,
stretch forth thy right hand to help
and defend us: through Christ our Lord. Amen.

Orlando Gibbons
1583-1625

www.thecatholicchoirbook.com • the anthology I copying & sharing of this music is permitted under creative commons 3.0

copying & sharing of this music is permitted under creative commons 3.0 • the anthology I • www.thecatholicchoirbook.com

 copying & sharing of this music is permitted under creative commons 3.0

copying & sharing of this music is permitted under creative commons 3.0 • the anthology I • www.thecatholicchoirbook.com

www.thecatholicchoirbook.com • the anthology I copying & sharing of this music is permitted under creative commons 3.0

copying & sharing of this music is permitted under creative commons 3.0 • the anthology I • www.thecatholicchoirbook.com

ANGELUS AUTEM DOMINI

1 Chronicles 21

*The Angel of the Lord came down from heaven, and rolled away the stone,
and sat upon it; and said to the women, "Do not be afraid;
you seek him who was crucified: he is risen, come and see
the place where the Lord's body was." Alleluia, alleluia, alleluia.*

Felice Anerio
1560-1614

 copying & sharing of this music is permitted under creative commons 3.0

copying & sharing of this music is permitted under creative commons 3.0 • the anthology I • www.thecatholicchoirbook.com

 copying & sharing of this music is permitted under creative commons 3.0

26
fí - xum quáe - ri - tis. Jam re - sur - ré - xit,
- - a cru - ci - fí - xum quáe - ri - tis. Jam re - sur - ré - xit,
fí - xum quáe - - - - ri - tis. Jam re - sur -
fí - - - - - - xum quáe - ri - tis. Jam re - sur -
26
31
jam re - sur - ré - - - - - xit: Ve - ní - te et vi - dé - te
jam re - sur - ré - - - - - xit: Ve - ní - te et vi - dé - te
ré - xit, jam re - sur - ré - xit: Ve - ní - te et vi - dé - te
ré - xit, jam re - sur - ré - xit: Ve - ní - te et vi - dé - te
31

 copying & sharing of this music is permitted under creative commons 3.0

ASSUMPTA EST MARIA

Vespers of the Assumption

Mary is taken up into heaven,
the Angels rejoice,
praising, they bless God.Mary the Virgin is taken up
into the heavenly chamber,
in which the King of kings sits upon His starry throne.

Peter Philips
1561-1628

copying & sharing of this music is permitted under creative commons 3.0 • the anthology I • www.thecatholicchoirbook.com

 copying & sharing of this music is permitted under creative commons 3.0

copying & sharing of this music is permitted under creative commons 3.0 • the anthology I • www.thecatholicchoirbook.com

www.thecatholicchoirbook.com • the anthology I copying & sharing of this music is permitted under creative commons 3.0

39
mum, ad ae-the-re-um tha - la-mum, in quo Rex re - gum
ad ae-the-re-um tha - la-mum, in quo Rex re - gum
39
mum, ad ae-the-re-um tha - la-mum, in quo Rex re -
mum, ad ae-the-re-um tha - la-mum, in quo Rex re - gum in quo Rex re -
mum, in quo Rex re - gum
39
44
in quo Rex re - gum stel - la - to se-det so - li-o, stel-
stel - la - to se - det so - li-o,
44
gum in quo Rex re-gum stel - la - to se - det so - li-o,
gum in quo Rex re - gum stel - la - to se-det so - li-o, stel-
in quo Rex re - gum stel - la - to se-det so - li-o, stel-
44

www.thecatholicchoirbook.com • the anthology I copying & sharing of this music is permitted under creative commons 3.0

copying & sharing of this music is permitted under creative commons 3.0

AVE MARIA

Hail Mary, full of grace, the Lord is with thee;
blessed art thou amongst women,
and blessed is the fruit of thy womb, Jesus.
Holy Mary, Mother of God, pray for us sinners now
and at the hour of our death. Amen.

Jacob Arcadelt
c.1505-c.1568

Arranger: Pierre-Louis Dietsch
1808-1865

S
A
T
B
A - ve Ma - ri - a, gra - ti - a ple - na,
Do - mi - nus te - cum, a - ve Ma - ri - a.

 copying & sharing of this music is permitted under creative commons 3.0

copying & sharing of this music is permitted under creative commons 3.0 • the anthology I • www.thecatholicchoirbook.com

 copying & sharing of this music is permitted under creative commons 3.0

25
ri - a, o - ra, o - ra pro no - bis, san - cta Ma - ri - a,
ri - a, o - ra, o - ra pro no - bis, san - cta Ma - ri - a,
ri - a, o - ra, o - ra pro no - bis, san - cta Ma - ri - a,
ri - a, o - ra, o - ra pro no - bis, san - cta Ma - ri - a,
30
o ra, o - ra pro no - bis. A - - - men.
o - ra, o - ra pro no - bis. A - - - men.
o - ra, o - ra pro no - bis. A - - - men.
o - ra, o - ra pro no - bis. A - - - men.

AVE MARIA

Robert Parsons
1535-1572

Hail Mary,
full of grace,
The Lord is with thee.
Blessed art thou among women,
and blessed is the fruit of thy womb, Jesus.
Holy Mary,
Mother of God,
pray for us sinners now,
and at the hour of death.
Amen.

 copying & sharing of this music is permitted under creative commons 3.0

copying & sharing of this music is permitted under creative commons 3.0 • the anthology I • www.thecatholicchoirbook.com

 copying & sharing of this music is permitted under creative commons 3.0

copying & sharing of this music is permitted under creative commons 3.0 • the anthology I • www.thecatholicchoirbook.com

 copying & sharing of this music is permitted under creative commons 3.0

copying & sharing of this music is permitted under creative commons 3.0 • the anthology I • www.thecatholicchoirbook.com

 copying & sharing of this music is permitted under creative commons 3.0

copying & sharing of this music is permitted under creative commons 3.0 • the anthology I • www.thecatholicchoirbook.com

 copying & sharing of this music is permitted under creative commons 3.0

69
A
72
men, A - men.
men.
men, A - men.
men.
men, a - men.

AVE MARIA

Hail Mary,
full of grace,
The Lord is with thee.
Blessed art thou among women,
and blessed is the fruit of thy womb, Jesus.
Holy Mary,

Anton Bruckner
1824-1896

 copying & sharing of this music is permitted under creative commons 3.0

copying & sharing of this music is permitted under creative commons 3.0 • the anthology I • www.thecatholicchoirbook.com

 copying & sharing of this music is permitted under creative commons 3.0

26
ri - a, ma - ter De - - - - - - - - - i,
ri - a, ma - ter De - - - - - - - - - i,
ma - - - - - - ter De - - - - - - - - - i.
p
ri - a, ma - ter De - - - - - - - - - i, o - ra
26
31
dim.
o - ra pro no - bis pec - ca - to - - - - - - ri -
dim.
o - ra pro no - bis pec - ca - to - - - - - - ri -
p o - ra pro no - bis
dim.
p
o - ra pro no - bis pec - ca - to - - - - - - ri -
dim.
o - ra pro no - bis pec - ca - to - - - - - - ri -
31

36
bus, nunc et in ho - - ra mor - tis no - strae
bus, nunc et in ho - - ra mor - tis no - strae
bus, nunc et in ho - - ra mor - tis no - strae
bus, nunc et in ho - - ra mor - tis no - strae
36
41
mor - tis no - strae, San - cta Ma - ri - a, o - ra pro
mor - tis no - strae, San - cta Ma - ri - a, o - ra pro
mor - tis no - strae, San - cta Ma - ri - a, o - ra pro
mor - tis no - strae, San - cta Ma - ri - a, o - ra pro
41

 copying & sharing of this music is permitted under creative commons 3.0

copying & sharing of this music is permitted under creative commons 3.0 • the anthology I • www.thecatholicchoirbook.com

AVE MARIA

Hail Mary,
full of grace,
The Lord is with thee.
Blessed art thou among women,
and blessed is the fruit of thy womb, Jesus.
Holy Mary,
Mother of God,
pray for us sinners now,
and at the hour of death.
Amen.

William Byrd
1540-1623

www.thecatholicchoirbook.com • the anthology I copying & sharing of this music is permitted under creative commons 3.0

copying & sharing of this music is permitted under creative commons 3.0 • the anthology I • www.thecatholicchoirbook.com

 copying & sharing of this music is permitted under creative commons 3.0

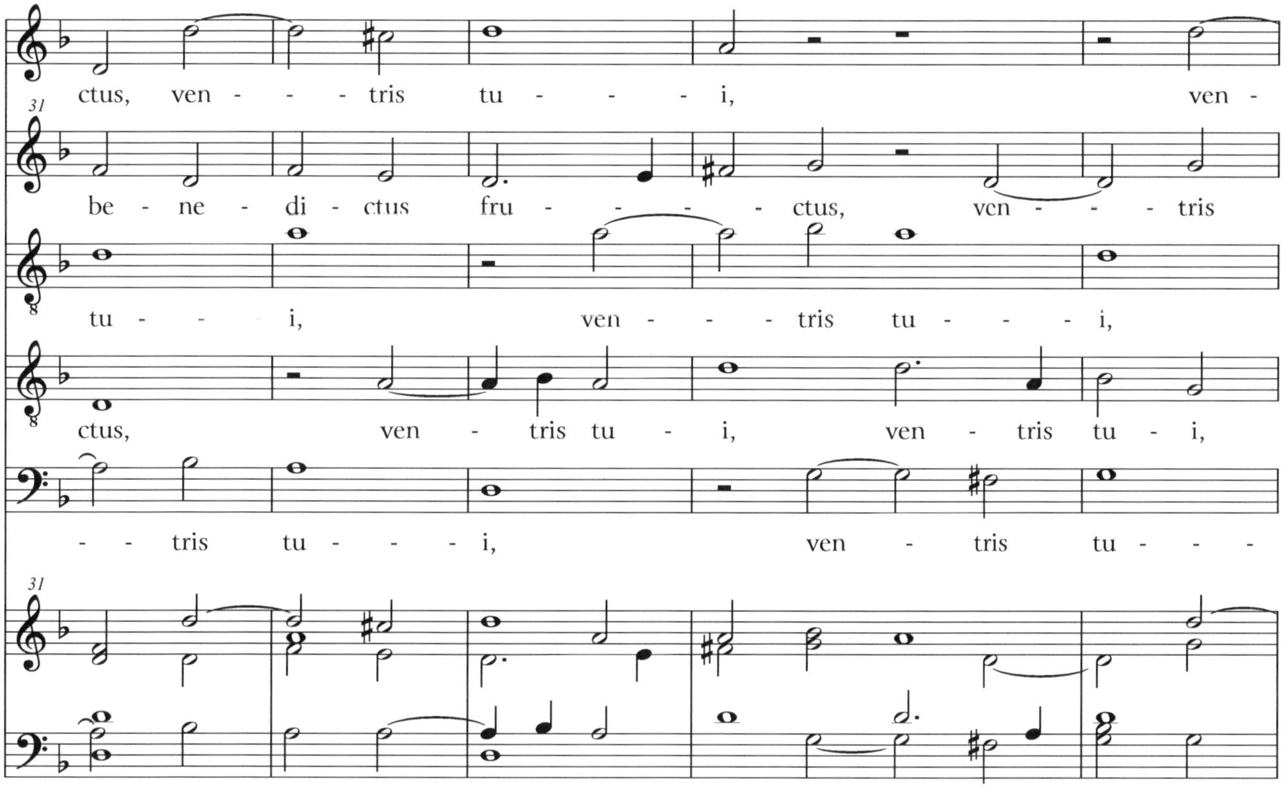

copying & sharing of this music is permitted under creative commons 3.0 • the anthology I • www.thecatholicchoirbook.com

 copying & sharing of this music is permitted under creative commons 3.0

copying & sharing of this music is permitted under creative commons 3.0 • the anthology I • www.thecatholicchoirbook.com

 copying & sharing of this music is permitted under creative commons 3.0

AVE MARIA

Giacomo Fogliano
1473-1548

Hail Mary,
full of grace,
The Lord is with thee.
Blessed art thou among women,
and blessed is the fruit of thy womb, Jesus.
Holy Mary,
Mother of God,
pray for us sinners now,
and at the hour of death.
Amen.

copying & sharing of this music is permitted under creative commons 3.0 • the anthology I • www.thecatholicchoirbook.com

 copying & sharing of this music is permitted under creative commons 3.0

copying & sharing of this music is permitted under creative commons 3.0 • the anthology I • www.thecatholicchoirbook.com

 copying & sharing of this music is permitted under creative commons 3.0

copying & sharing of this music is permitted under creative commons 3.0 • the anthology I • www.thecatholicchoirbook.com

AVE MARIA

Hail Mary,
full of grace,
The Lord is with thee.
Blessed art thou among women,
and blessed is the fruit of thy womb, Jesus.
Holy Mary,
Mother of God,
pray for us sinners now,
and at the hour of death.
Amen.

Francisco Guerrero
1528–1599

 copying & sharing of this music is permitted under creative commons 3.0

copying & sharing of this music is permitted under creative commons 3.0 • the anthology I • www.thecatholicchoirbook.com

 copying & sharing of this music is permitted under creative commons 3.0

copying & sharing of this music is permitted under creative commons 3.0 • the anthology I • www.thecatholicchoirbook.com

 copying & sharing of this music is permitted under creative commons 3.0

37
- - - i, Jé - - - - - - sus,
Jé - sus, vén - tris tú -
et be - ne - dí - ctus frú - - - ctus
et be - ne - dí - ctus frú - - - ctus
37
41
frú - ctus vén - tris tú -
i, frú - ctus vén - tris tú - - - i, frú -
vén - tris tú - - - i, Jé - - - sus, frú - ctus
vén - - - - - - - tris tú - - - - - - i, frú - ctus
41

 copying & sharing of this music is permitted under creative commons 3.0

53
gí - na caé - - - - - li. O má - ter Dé -
re - gí - na caé - - - - - li. O má - ter Dé -
gí - na caé - li, re - gí - na caé - li. O má - ter Dé -
gí - na caé - - - - - li. O má - ter Dé - - - - -
53
57
- - - i, ó - ra pro - nó -
i, ó - ra pro nó - - - bis pec - ca - tó - ri -
i, ó - ra pro nó - bis pec - ca - tó - - - - ri -
i, ó - ra pro nó - bis pec - - - ca - tó - ri -
57

 copying & sharing of this music is permitted under creative commons 3.0

copying & sharing of this music is permitted under creative commons 3.0 • the anthology I • www.thecatholicchoirbook.com

AVE REGINA COELORUM

Marian Antiphon
Fr. Edward Caswall 1814-1878
Translation

Hail, O Queen of Heav'n enthron'd,
Hail, by angels Mistress own'd
Root of Jesse, Gate of morn,
Whence the world's true light was born.
Glorious Virgin, joy to thee,
Lovliest whom in Heaven they see,
Fairest thou where all are fair!
Plead with Christ our sins to spare.

Guillaume Dufay
c.1400-1474

www.thecatholicchoirbook.com • the anthology I copying & sharing of this music is permitted under creative commons 3.0

copying & sharing of this music is permitted under creative commons 3.0 • the anthology I • www.thecatholicchoirbook.com

 copying & sharing of this music is permitted under creative commons 3.0

34
bis sem - per Chri - - - - stum ex - o - - - - ra.
bis sem - per Chri - - - stum ex - o - - - - ra. Al -
bis sem - per Chri - - - stum ex - o - - - - ra.
34

40
Al - - - le - - - - - - - - - lu - - - - - - ya.
- - - le - - - - - - - - - lu - - - - - - ya.
Al - - - le - - - - - - - - - lu - - - - - - ya.
40

copying & sharing of this music is permitted under creative commons 3.0 • the anthology I • www.thecatholicchoirbook.com

AVE VERUM

Pope Innocent VI
d 1362

Edward Elgar
1857-1934

Für uns der rechte Mann/Den Gott hat selbst erkoren+

Largo
p
S
1
A - ve ve - rum cor - pus na - tum Ex Ma - ri - a Vir - gi - ne, Ve - re
Je - su, Word of God In - car - nate, Of the Vir - gin Ma - ry born, On the
6
pas - sum, im - mo - la - tum In cru - ce pro ho - mi - ne.
Cross Thy sa - cred Bod - y For us men with nails was torn.

 copying & sharing of this music is permitted under creative commons 3.0

A - ve ve - rum cor - pus na - tum Ex Ma - ri - a Vir - gi -
Je - su, Word of God In - car - nate, Of the Vir - gin Ma - ry
ne, Ve - re pas - sum, im - mo - la - tum In cru - ce pro ho - mi - ne.
born, On the Cross Thy sa - cred Bod - y For us men with nails was torn.

copying & sharing of this music is permitted under creative commons 3.0 •

 copying & sharing of this music is permitted under creative commons 3.0

copying & sharing of this music is permitted under creative commons 3.0 • the anthology I • www.thecatholicchoirbook.com

39
f
pp
dul - cis Je - su, Fi - li Ma - ri - - - ae,
Je - su, hear us, Son of Ma - - - ry,
dul - cis Je - su Fi - li Ma - ri - - - ae, Ma - ri - ae.
Je - su, hear us, Son of Ma - - - ry, of Ma - ry.
dul - cis Je - su Fi - li Ma - ri - - - ae, Ma - ri - ae.
Je - su, hear us, Son of Ma - - - ry, of Ma - ry.
dul - cis Je - su, Fi - li Ma - ri - - - ae, Ma - ri - ae.
Je - su, hear us, Son of Ma - - - ry, of Ma - ry.
39
f
pp

 copying & sharing of this music is permitted under creative commons 3.0

AVE VERUM

Pope Innocent VI
d. 1362

Hail the true body, born of the Virgin Mary:
You who truly suffered and were sacrificed
on the cross for the sake of man.
From whose pierced flank flowed water and blood:
Be a foretaste for us in the trial of death.
O sweet, O gentle, O Jesu, son of Mary, have mercy on me.

William Byrd
1540-1623

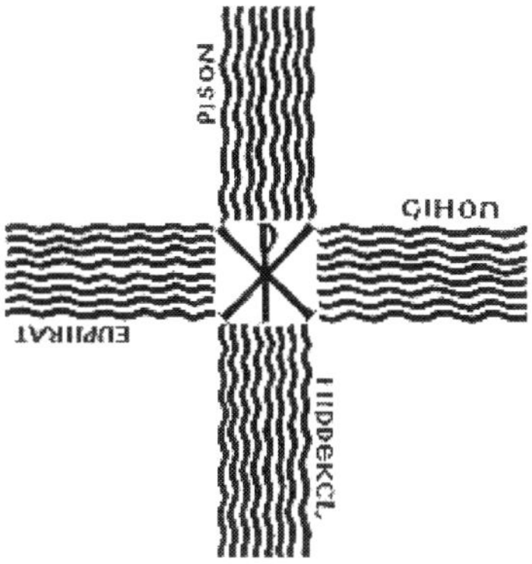

Die vier Paradiesströme +

copying & sharing of this music is permitted under creative commons 3.0 • the anthology I • www.thecatholicchoirbook.com

 copying & sharing of this music is permitted under creative commons 3.0

16
jus lá - tus per - fo-rá - - - tum, ún - da flú - xit sán - gui-
jus lá - tus per - fo - rá - tum, ún - da flú - xit sán - gui-
jus lá - tus per - fo - rá - tum, ún - da
jus lá - tus per - for - rá - tum, ún - da flú -
16

21
ne, sán - gui - ne. É - sto nó - bis prae - gu - stá - tum in
ne, sán - gui - ne. É - sto nó - bis prae - gu - stá - tum in
flú - xit sán - gui - ne. É - sto nó - - bis prae - gu - stá - tum in
xit sán - gui - ne. É - sto nó - bis prae - gu - stá - tum
21

copying & sharing of this music is permitted under creative commons 3.0 • the anthology I • www.thecatholicchoirbook.com

 copying & sharing of this music is permitted under creative commons 3.0

copying & sharing of this music is permitted under creative commons 3.0 • the anthology I • www.thecatholicchoirbook.com

 copying & sharing of this music is permitted under creative commons 3.0

56
mé - i, mé - - - - - i. A - - - - men.
ré - re mé - - - - - - i. A - - - - - - - - men.
i, mi - se - ré - re mé - i. A - - - - - - - - men.
se - ré - re mé - - - - - i. A - - - - - men.
56

copying & sharing of this music is permitted under creative commons 3.0 • the anthology I • www.thecatholicchoirbook.com

AVE VERUM

Pope Innocent VI
d 1362

Wolfgang Amadeus Mozart
1756-1791

Hail the true body, born of the Virgin Mary:
You who truly suffered and were sacrificed
on the cross for the sake of man.
From whose pierced flank flowed water and blood:
Be a foretaste for us in the trial of death.
O sweet, O gentle, O Jesu, son of Mary, have mercy on me.

www.thecatholicchoirbook.com • the anthology I copying & sharing of this music is permitted under creative commons 3.0

copying & sharing of this music is permitted under creative commons 3.0 • the anthology I • www.thecatholicchoirbook.com

 copying & sharing of this music is permitted under creative commons 3.0

copying & sharing of this music is permitted under creative commons 3.0 • the anthology I • www.thecatholicchoirbook.com

26
un - da flu - xit et san - - - gui ne, es - to
un - da flu - xit et san - - - gui ne, es - to
un - da flu - xit et san - - - gui ne,
un - da flu - xit et san - - - gui ne,
26
31
no - bis prae - gus - ta - tum in mor - - - - - - tis ex -
no - bis prae - gus - ta - tum in mor - - - - - - tis ex -
es - - - - to no - bis prae - gus - ta - tum in mor - tis ex -
es - - - - to no - bis prae - gus - ta - tum in mor - tis ex -
31

 copying & sharing of this music is permitted under creative commons 3.0

BEATI QUORUM VIA

Psalm 119:1

Blessed are the undefiled in the way,
who walk in the law of the Lord.

Charles Villiers Stanford
1852-1924

copying & sharing of this music is permitted under creative commons 3.0 • the anthology I • www.thecatholicchoirbook.com

 copying & sharing of this music is permitted under creative commons 3.0

17
cresc.
dim.
Be - á - ti quó-rum ví - a ín-te-gra est, ví - a
17
cresc.
dim.
Be - á - ti quó-rum ví - a ín-te-gra est, quó-rum ví - - - a
cresc.
dim.
Be - á - ti quó-rum ví - a ín-te-gra est, quó-rum ví - - - a
cresc.
dim.
8
quó-rum ví - - - - a ín-te-gra est, ví - a
cresc.
dim.
quó-rum ví - - - - a ín-te-gra est, quó-rum ví - a
cresc.
dim.
quó-rum ví - - - - a ín-te-gra est, quó-rum ví - a
17

 copying & sharing of this music is permitted under creative commons 3.0

copying & sharing of this music is permitted under creative commons 3.0 • the anthology I • www.thecatholicchoirbook.com

 copying & sharing of this music is permitted under creative commons 3.0

copying & sharing of this music is permitted under creative commons 3.0 • the anthology I • www.thecatholicchoirbook.com

 copying & sharing of this music is permitted under creative commons 3.0

copying & sharing of this music is permitted under creative commons 3.0 • the anthology I • www.thecatholicchoirbook.com

 copying & sharing of this music is permitted under creative commons 3.0

85
ám - bu - lant in lé - ge Dó - mi - ni Dó - mi - ni.
85
lé - - - ge, in lé - ge Dó - mi - ni Dó - mi - ni.
ni, in lé - ge Dó - mi - ni, Dó - mi - ni.
ni, in lé - ge Dó - mi - ni.
ni, in lé - ge Dó - mi - ni.
ni, in lé - ge Dó - mi - ni.
85

CANTATE DOMINO

Psalm 98

O sing unto the Lord a new song:
let the congregation of saints praise him.
Let Israel rejoice in him that made him:
and let the children of Sion be joyful in their King.

Giuseppi Pitoni
1657-1743

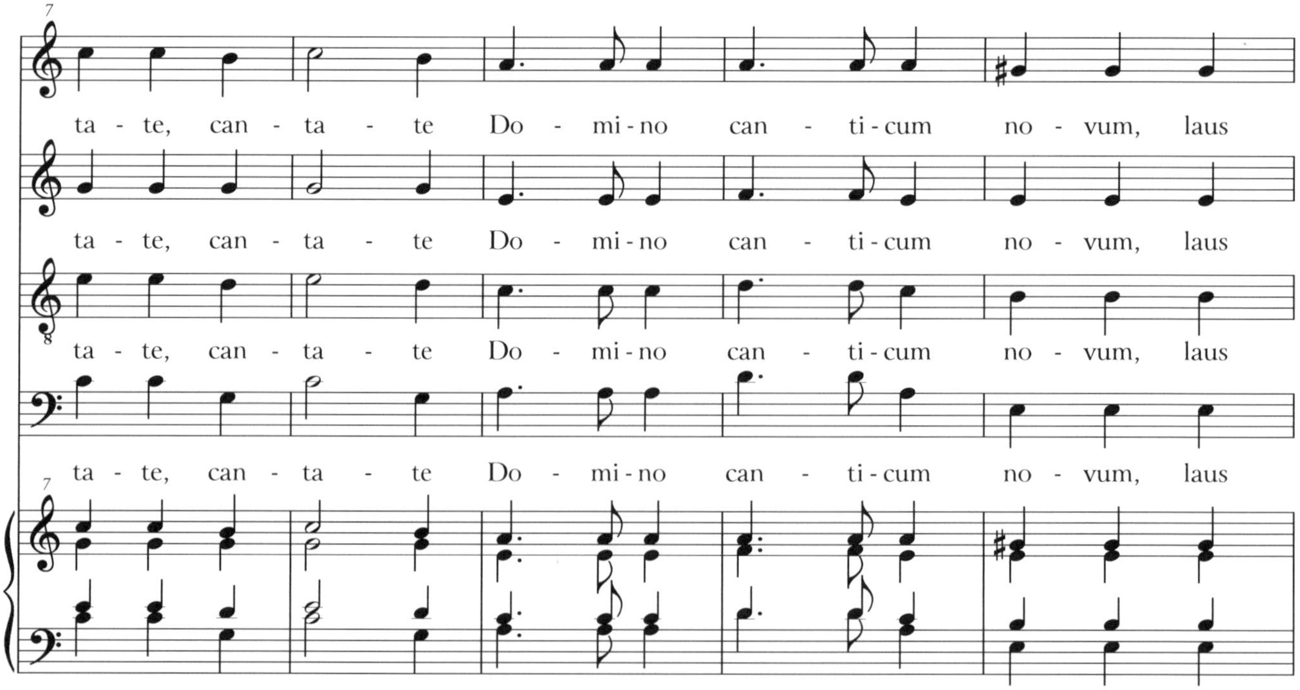

 copying & sharing of this music is permitted under creative commons 3.0

copying & sharing of this music is permitted under creative commons 3.0 • the anthology I • www.thecatholicchoirbook.com

24
te - tur, lae - te - tur in e - o, qui fe - cit e -
te - tur, lae - te - tur in e - o, qui fe - cit e -
te - tur, lae - te - tur in e - o, qui fe - cit e -
te - tur, lae - te - tur in e - o, qui fe - cit e -
24
30
um, et fi - li - i Si - on, et fi - li - i Si - on, ex - ul - tent,
um, et fi - li - i Si - on, et fi - li - i Si - on, ex -
um, et fi - li - i Si - on, et fi - li - i Si - on, ex -
um, et fi - li - i Si - on, et fi - li - i Si - on, ex - ul - tent,
30

 copying & sharing of this music is permitted under creative commons 3.0

36
ex - - - - ul - tent, ex - ul - tent in re - ge su -
ul - tent, ex - ul - tent in re - ge su -
ul - tent, ex - ul - tent in re - ge su -
ex - ul - tent, ex - ul - tent in re - ge su -
36
41
o, ex - ul - tent, ex - ul - tent in re - ge su - o.
o, ex - ul - tent, ex - ul - tent in re - ge su - o.
o, ex - ul - tent, ex - ul - tent in re - ge su - o.
o, ex - ul - tent, ex - ul - tent in re - ge su - o.
41

copying & sharing of this music is permitted under creative commons 3.0 • the anthology I • www.thecatholicchoirbook.com

CANTATE DOMINO

Psalm 98

O sing unto the Lord a new song:
let the congregation of saints praise him.
Let Israel rejoice in him that made him:
and let the children of Sion be joyful in their King.

Hans Leo Hassler
c. 25 October 1564-1612

 copying & sharing of this music is permitted under creative commons 3.0

copying & sharing of this music is permitted under creative commons 3.0 • the anthology I • www.thecatholicchoirbook.com

 copying & sharing of this music is permitted under creative commons 3.0

copying & sharing of this music is permitted under creative commons 3.0 • the anthology I • www.thecatholicchoirbook.com

42
bí - - - - - li - a é - jus, mi - ra - bí - li - a é - jus.
bí - li - a é - jus, mi - ra - bí - li - a é - jus.
bí - li - a é - - - - jus, mi - ra - bí - li - a é - jus.
bí - - - li - a é - jus, mi - ra - bí - li - a é - jus.
42

 copying & sharing of this music is permitted under creative commons 3.0

CANTATE DOMINO

Psalm 97

O sing unto the Lord a new song:
let the congregation of saints praise him.
Let Israel rejoice in him that made him:
and let the children of Sion be joyful in their King.

Daniel Friderici
1584-1638

copying & sharing of this music is permitted under creative commons 3.0 • the anthology I • www.thecatholicchoirbook.com

9
qui - a mi-ra - bi - li - a fe - - - - - - - - - - cit.
qui - a mi-ra - bi - li - a fe - - - - - - - - - - cit.
qui - a mi-ra - bi - li - a fe - - - - - - - - - - cit.
9

15
Sal - va - vit dex - te - ra tu - a in bra - chi - o, in
Sal - va - vit dex - te - ra tu - a in bra - chi - o, in
Sal - va - vit dex - te - ra tu - a in bra - chi - o, in
15

 copying & sharing of this music is permitted under creative commons 3.0

19
bra - chi-o, in bra - chi-o san - cto su - o, su - - - - - -
bra - chi-o, in bra - chi-o san - cto su - o, su - - - - - - -
bra - chi-o, in bra - chi-o san - cto su - o, su - - - - - - -
19
23
- - - - - - - o, bra - chi - o san - cto su - - o.
- - - - - - - o, bra - chi - o san - cto su - o.
- - - - - - - o, bra - chi - o san - cto su - - o.
23

copying & sharing of this music is permitted under creative commons 3.0 • the anthology I • www.thecatholicchoirbook.com

CANTATE DOMINO

Psalm 97

O sing unto the Lord a new song:
let the congregation of saints praise him.
Let Israel rejoice in him that made him:
and let the children of Sion be joyful in their King.

Giovanni Andrea Cima
c.1580-after 1627

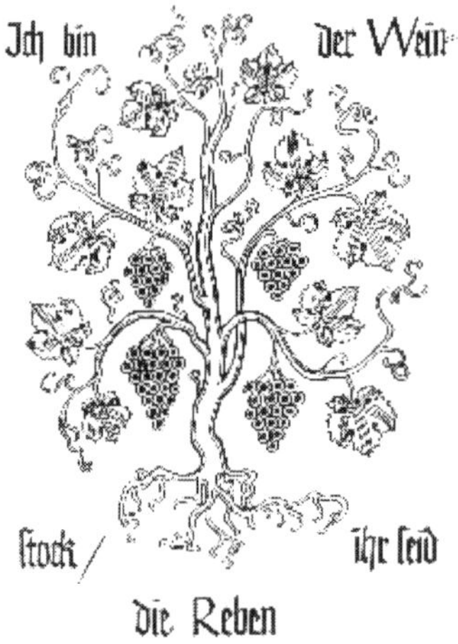

 copying & sharing of this music is permitted under creative commons 3.0

copying & sharing of this music is permitted under creative commons 3.0 • the anthology I • www.thecatholicchoirbook.com

 copying & sharing of this music is permitted under creative commons 3.0

16
be - ne - di - ci - te no - mi - ni e - - - ius
an - nun - ci - a - te, an - nun - ci -
16
be - ne - di - ci - te no - mi - ni e - ius,
16
19
an -
a - te de di - e in di - em, de di - e in di - em sa - lu - ta - ris e - - -
19
19

copying & sharing of this music is permitted under creative commons 3.0 • the anthology I • www.thecatholicchoirbook.com

22
nun - - ci - a - te, an - nun - ci - a - te in - ter gen - tes no - mi - ni
ius
22
22
25
in om - ni - bus po - pu - lis, in om - ni - bus po - pu - lis mi - ra - bi - li - a
e - ius in om - ni - bus po - pu - lis, in om - ni - bus po - pu - lis mi - ra - bi - li - a e -
in om - ni - bus po - pu - lis, in om - ni - bus po - pu - lis mi - ra - bi - li - a
25
in om - ni - bus po - pu - lis, in om - ni - bus po - pu - lis mi - ra -
25

 copying & sharing of this music is permitted under creative commons 3.0

28
e - ius, mi-ra-bi - li-a e - ius mi-ra-bi - - - li-a e -
ius mi-ra-bi - - - li-a e - ius e - - - - -
e - ius mi-ra-bi-li-a e - ius, mi-ra-bi-li-a e -
28
bi-li-a e - ius, mi-ra-bi-li-a e - ius, mi-ra-bi-li-a e - - -
28
33
ius. Al - - - - - - - - - - le - lu-ia.
ius al - - - - -
ius
33
ius.
33

copying & sharing of this music is permitted under creative commons 3.0 • the anthology I • www.thecatholicchoirbook.com

 copying & sharing of this music is permitted under creative commons 3.0

47
al - le - lu - ia. Al - le - - - lu - ia.
al - le - lu - ia, al - le - lu - ia, al - le -
al - le - lu - ia, al - le - - - lu - ia,
47
- - - lu - ia. al - le - lu - ia, Al - le -
47
50
al - le - lu - ia, al - le - lu - ia. Al - le - lu - - - ia.
- lu - ia, al - le - lu - ia, al - - - - le - lu - - - - - - ia.
al - le - lu - ia, al - le - lu - ia, al - le - lu - ia, al - le - lu ia.
50
- lu - ia. Al - le - lu - ia. Al - - - le - lu - - - - - - ia.
50

CANTATE DOMINO

Psalm 97

O sing unto the Lord a new song:
let the congregation of saints praise him.
Let Israel rejoice in him that made him:
and let the children of Sion be joyful in their King.

Giovanni Croce
1557-1609

Das Kreuz im Herzen der Rose / Das Wappenbild Luthers

www.thecatholicchoirbook.com • the anthology I copying & sharing of this music is permitted under creative commons 3.0

copying & sharing of this music is permitted under creative commons 3.0 • the anthology I • www.thecatholicchoirbook.com

 copying & sharing of this music is permitted under creative commons 3.0

21
Do - mi - no et be - ne - di - ci - te no - mi - ni e - jus.
Do - mi - no et be - ne - di - ci - te no - mi - ni e - jus.
Do - mi - no et be - ne - di - ci - te no - mi - ni e - jus.
Do - mi - no et be - ne - di - ci - te no - mi - ni e - jus.
21
27
An - nun - ti - a - - te,
An - nun - ci - a - te de di - e,
An - nun - ti - a - - - te de di - - e, an -
An - nun - ti - a - - - te de di - - e, an -
27

 copying & sharing of this music is permitted under creative commons 3.0

copying & sharing of this music is permitted under creative commons 3.0 • the anthology I • www.thecatholicchoirbook.com

 copying & sharing of this music is permitted under creative commons 3.0

CANTATE DOMINO

Psalm 97

O sing unto the Lord a new song:
let the congregation of saints praise him.
Let Israel rejoice in him that made him:
and let the children of Sion be joyful in their King.

Wolfgang Amadeus Mozart
1756-1791

S
A
T
B
Can-ta-te Do-mi-no om - nis ter - ra,
can - ta - - - - - - - - - - - - - te,

copying & sharing of this music is permitted under creative commons 3.0 • the anthology I • www.thecatholicchoirbook.com

7
can ta - te Do - mi - no om - nis ter - ra, can - ta - te.
7
7
10
Can-ta - te Do - mi-no om - - - nis ter - - ra,
Can-ta - te Do - mi-no om - - nis
Can-ta - te Do - mi-no
10
10

 copying & sharing of this music is permitted under creative commons 3.0

13
can - ta - - - - - - - - - - - - - - te,
ter - - - ra, can - ta - - - - - - - - - - - -
om - - - nis ter - ra, can - ta - - -
13
Can-ta-te Do - mi-no om - nis ter - ra,
13
16
can-ta-te-Do - mi-no om - nis ter - ra, can - ta - te.
- - - - te, can-ta-te-Do - mi-no om - nis ter - ra, can-
- - - - - - - - - - - - - - te, can-ta-te-Do - mi-
16
can - ta - - - - - - - - - - - - - - te,
16

copying & sharing of this music is permitted under creative commons 3.0 • the anthology I • www.thecatholicchoirbook.com

19
ta - te.
no om - nis ter - ra, can - ta - te.
19
can - ta - te - Do - mi - no om - nis ter - ra, can - ta - te.
19

 copying & sharing of this music is permitted under creative commons 3.0

CRUCIFIXUS

Nicene Creed

Crucified for us, under Pontius Pilate:
suffered and was buried.

Antonio Lotti
1667-1740

 copying & sharing of this music is permitted under creative commons 3.0

12
cru - ci - fí - xus é - ti - am pro nó - bis
cru - ci - fí - xus é - ti - am pro nó - bis cru - ci - fí - xus
cru - ci - fí - xus é - ti - am pro nó - - - bis
cru - ci - fí - xus é - ti - am pro nó - bis
cru - ci - fí - xus é - ti - am pro nó - - - - - bis,
cru - ci - fí - xus é - ti - am pro nó - - - bis cru - ci - fí - xus
cru - ci - fí - xus é - ti - am pro nó - bis
cru - ci - fí - xus é - ti - am pro nó - bis, cru - - - ci - - - fí - xus
12
12

 copying & sharing of this music is permitted under creative commons 3.0

copying & sharing of this music is permitted under creative commons 3.0 • the anthology I • www.thecatholicchoirbook.com

 copying & sharing of this music is permitted under creative commons 3.0

copying & sharing of this music is permitted under creative commons 3.0 • the anthology I • www.thecatholicchoirbook.com

 copying & sharing of this music is permitted under creative commons 3.0

35
- - - - - - - - tus et se - púl - - - tus est.
- - - - - - - tus et se - púl - - - tus est.
- - - - - - - - tus et se - púl - - - - tus est.
- - - - - - - tus et se - púl - - - - tus est.
púl - - - - - - - tus et se - púl - - - tus est.
- - - - - - - tus et se - púl - - - - tus est.
- - - - - - - tus et se - púl - - - tus est.
- - - - - - - xus et se - púl - - - tus est.
35
35

CRUX FIDELIS

Saint Venantius Honorius Clementianus Fortunatus
c530-c609

King John IV of Portugal
1604-1656

Faithful cross, above all other,
One and only noble tree:
None in foliage, none in blossom,
None in fruit thy peer may be.
Sweetest wood and sweetest iron,
Sweetest weight is hung on thee!

 copying & sharing of this music is permitted under creative commons 3.0

copying & sharing of this music is permitted under creative commons 3.0 • the anthology I • www.thecatholicchoirbook.com

 copying & sharing of this music is permitted under creative commons 3.0

DOMINE DEUS, AGNUS DEI

Gloria, RV 588

Antonio Lucio Vivaldi
1678-1741

O Lord God, Lamb of God,
Son of the Father,
that takest away the sins of the world,
have mercy upon us.
Thou that takest away the sins of the world,
have mercy upon us.
Thou that takest away the sins of the world,
receive our prayer.

copying & sharing of this music is permitted under creative commons 3.0 • the anthology I • www.thecatholicchoirbook.com

 copying & sharing of this music is permitted under creative commons 3.0

copying & sharing of this music is permitted under creative commons 3.0 • the anthology I • www.thecatholicchoirbook.com

 copying & sharing of this music is permitted under creative commons 3.0

mi - se - re - re no - bis.
mi-se-re-re no - bis.
mi-se-re-re no - bis.
mi-se-re-re no - bis.
mi-se-re-re no - bis.

copying & sharing of this music is permitted under creative commons 3.0 • the anthology I • www.thecatholicchoirbook.com

GOD SO LOVED THE WORLD

W. J. Sparrow Simpson
1859-1952

John Goss
1800-1880

1
S
mf God so lov - ed the world, that He gave His on - ly be - got - ten
A
mf God so lov - ed the world, that He gave His on - ly be - got - ten
T
mf God so lov - ed the world, that He gave His on - ly be - got - ten
B
mf God so lov - ed the world, that He gave His on - ly be - got - ten
1

 copying & sharing of this music is permitted under creative commons 3.0

copying & sharing of this music is permitted under creative commons 3.0 • the anthology I • www.thecatholicchoirbook.com

 copying & sharing of this music is permitted under creative commons 3.0

GOD SO LOVED THE WORLD

From The Crucifixion

W. J. Sparrow Simpson
1859-1952

John Stainer
1840-1901

copying & sharing of this music is permitted under creative commons 3.0 • the anthology I • www.thecatholicchoirbook.com

 copying & sharing of this music is permitted under creative commons 3.0

copying & sharing of this music is permitted under creative commons 3.0 • the anthology I • www.thecatholicchoirbook.com

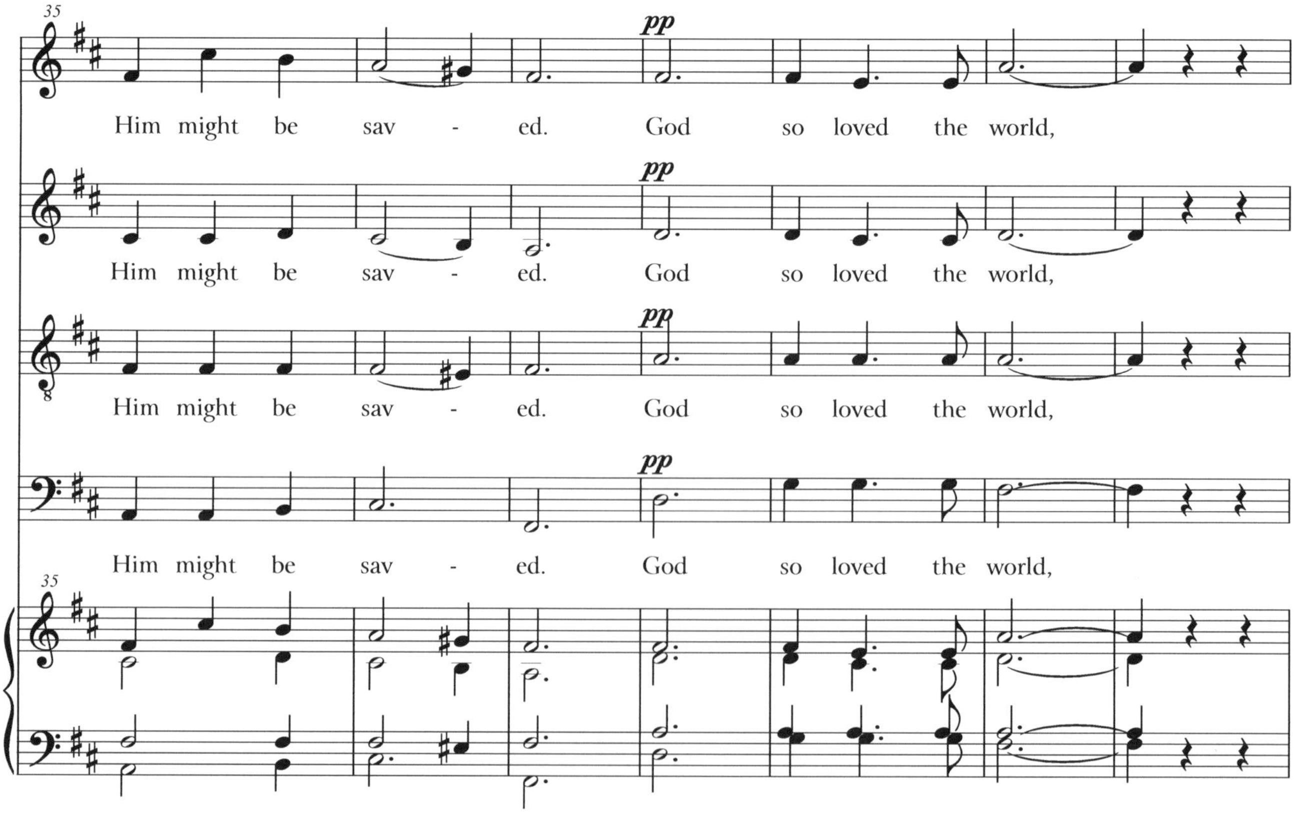

 copying & sharing of this music is permitted under creative commons 3.0

copying & sharing of this music is permitted under creative commons 3.0 • the anthology I • www.thecatholicchoirbook.com

 copying & sharing of this music is permitted under creative commons 3.0

copying & sharing of this music is permitted under creative commons 3.0 • the anthology I • www.thecatholicchoirbook.com

HEAR MY PRAYER, O LORD

Psalm 102.1, Book of Common Prayer

Henry Purcell
1659-1695

 copying & sharing of this music is permitted under creative commons 3.0

7
cry - ing come un - to thee, hear my pray-er, O
and let my cry - ing come un - to thee,
cry - ing come un - to thee, and let my cry - ing
cry - ing come un - to thee, hear my pray-er, O
and let my cry - ing come un -
Hear my pray-er, O Lord,
Lord, and let my
Hear my pray-er, O Lord,
7
7

 copying & sharing of this music is permitted under creative commons 3.0

17
and let my cry - - - ing come un - to thee,
Lord, and let my cry - ing come
and let my cry - - - ing come un - to thee,
cry - ing come un - to thee, hear my pray-er, O Lord,
come un - to thee, and let my cry - ing
hear my pray - er, O Lord,
hear my pray-er, O Lord, and let my
17
17

 copying & sharing of this music is permitted under creative commons 3.0

copying & sharing of this music is permitted under creative commons 3.0 • the anthology I • www.thecatholicchoirbook.com

 copying & sharing of this music is permitted under creative commons 3.0

HIDE NOT THOU THY FACE

Psalm 102:2

Richard Farrant
c. 1530-1580

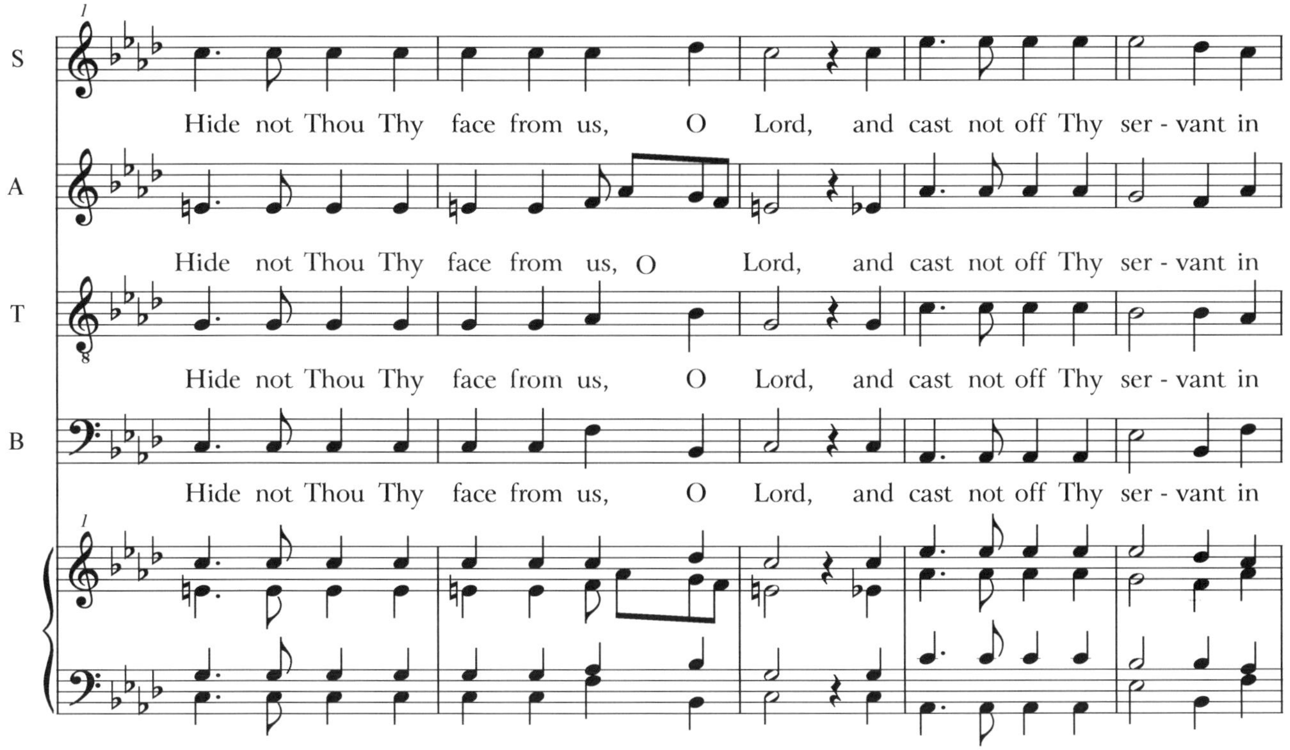

copying & sharing of this music is permitted under creative commons 3.0 • the anthology I • www.thecatholicchoirbook.com

12
our un - righ - te-ous - ness. For Thy mer - cies sake, for Thy mer - cies sake, de -
our un - righ - te - ous - ness. For Thy mer - cies sake, for Thy mer - cies sake, de -
our un - righ - te - ous - ness. For Thy mer - cies sake, for Thy mer - cies sake, de -
our un righ - te - ous: sins. For Thy mer - cies sake, for Thy mer - cies sake, de -
12
*
18
li - ver us from all our sins, de - li - ver us from all our sins.
li - ver us from all our sins, de - li - ver us from all our sins.
li - ver us from all our sins, de - li - ver us from all our sins.
li - ver us from all our sins, de - li - ver us from all our sins.
18

 copying & sharing of this music is permitted under creative commons 3.0

IF YE LOVE ME

Communion Antiphon
Sixth Sunday of Easter

Thomas Tallis
1505-1585

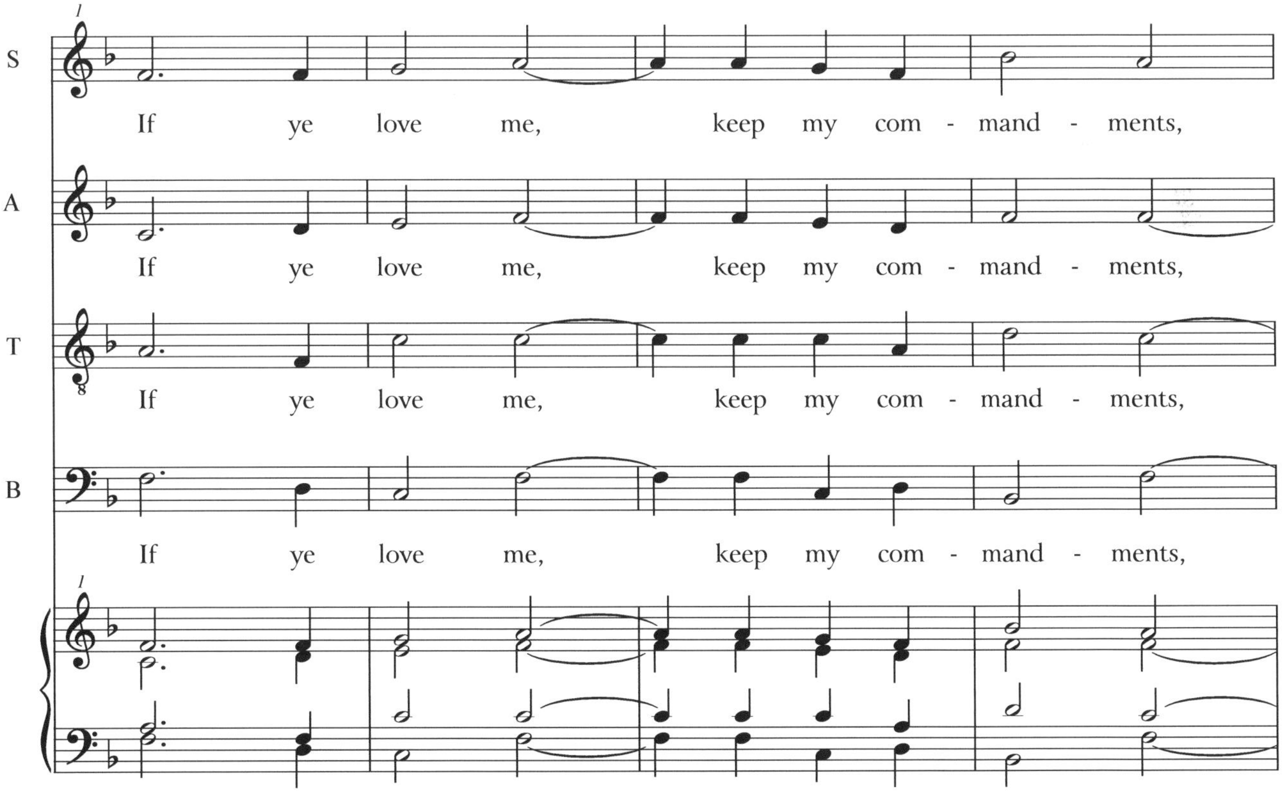
1
S
If ye love me, keep my com - mand - ments,
A
If ye love me, keep my com - mand - ments,
T
If ye love me, keep my com - mand - ments,
B
If ye love me, keep my com - mand - ments,
1

copying & sharing of this music is permitted under creative commons 3.0 • the anthology I • www.thecatholicchoirbook.com

 copying & sharing of this music is permitted under creative commons 3.0

13
er,
er, that he may
er, that he may bide with you for -
er, that he may bide with
13
16
that he may bide with you for - ev - er,
bide with you for - ev - er, with you for - ev - er, e'en
ev - er, that he may bide with you for - ev - er, e'en the
you for - ev - - - er, may bide with you for - ev - er, e'en
16

 copying & sharing of this music is permitted under creative commons 3.0

JESU DULCIS MEMORIA

Saint Bernard of Clairvaux
1090-1153

Jesus, sweet remembrance,
Granting the heart its true joys,
But above honey and all things
Is His sweet presence.

Tomás Luis de Victoria
1548-1611

copying & sharing of this music is permitted under creative commons 3.0 • the anthology I • www.thecatholicchoirbook.com

 copying & sharing of this music is permitted under creative commons 3.0

15
- mni - a, su - per mel et ó - mni - a E - jus dúl - cis
- - mni-a, su - - - per mel et ó - mni - a E - jus dúl -
- mni - a, su - per mel et ó - mni - a E - - jus
a, et ó - mni - a E -
15
20
præ - sén - - - - - ti - a, dúl - cis præ - sén - ti - a.
cis præ - sén - - - ti - a, dúl - cis præ - sén - ti - a.
dúl - cis præ - sén - - - ti - a, dúl - cis præ - sén - ti - a.
jus dúl - cis præ - sén - - - - - ti - - a.
20

JESU! REX ADMIRABILIS

St. Bernard of Clairvaux
1090-1153

Giovanni Pierluigi da Palestrina
1525-1594

Jesu, Prince ever-glorious!
Thou Lord of Hosts victorious!
Of radiance more than marvelous'
Master, be ruler over us!

Dwell, Lord, with us, and grant we may
Behold Thy light upon our way;
Scatter night's gloom, and so array
Earth, as heaven, in noon bright day.

1
S
Je - su! Rex ad - mi - ra - bi - lis et tri - um - pha - tor no - bi - lis
Ma - ne no - bis - cum Do - mi - ne et nos il - lus - tra lu - mi - ne,
A
Je - su! Rex ad - mi - ra - bi - lis et tri - um - pha - tor no - bi - lis
Ma - ne no - bis - cum Do - mi - ne et nos il - lus - tra lu - mi - ne,
B
Je - su! Rex ad - mi - ra - bi - lis et tri - um - pha - tor no - bi - lis
Ma - ne no - bis - cum Do - mi - ne et nos il - lus - tra lu - mi - ne,
1

 copying & sharing of this music is permitted under creative commons 3.0

copying & sharing of this music is permitted under creative commons 3.0 • the anthology I • www.thecatholicchoirbook.com

LOCUS ISTE

Gradual for the Dedication of a Church

This place was made by God,
a priceless sacrament;
beyond reproach.

Anton Bruckner
1824-1896

 copying & sharing of this music is permitted under creative commons 3.0

copying & sharing of this music is permitted under creative commons 3.0 • the anthology I • www.thecatholicchoirbook.com

 copying & sharing of this music is permitted under creative commons 3.0

copying & sharing of this music is permitted under creative commons 3.0 • the anthology I • www.thecatholicchoirbook.com

LORD, FOR THY TENDER MERCY'S SAKE

Lidley's Prayers
1566

Richard Farrant
1530-1580

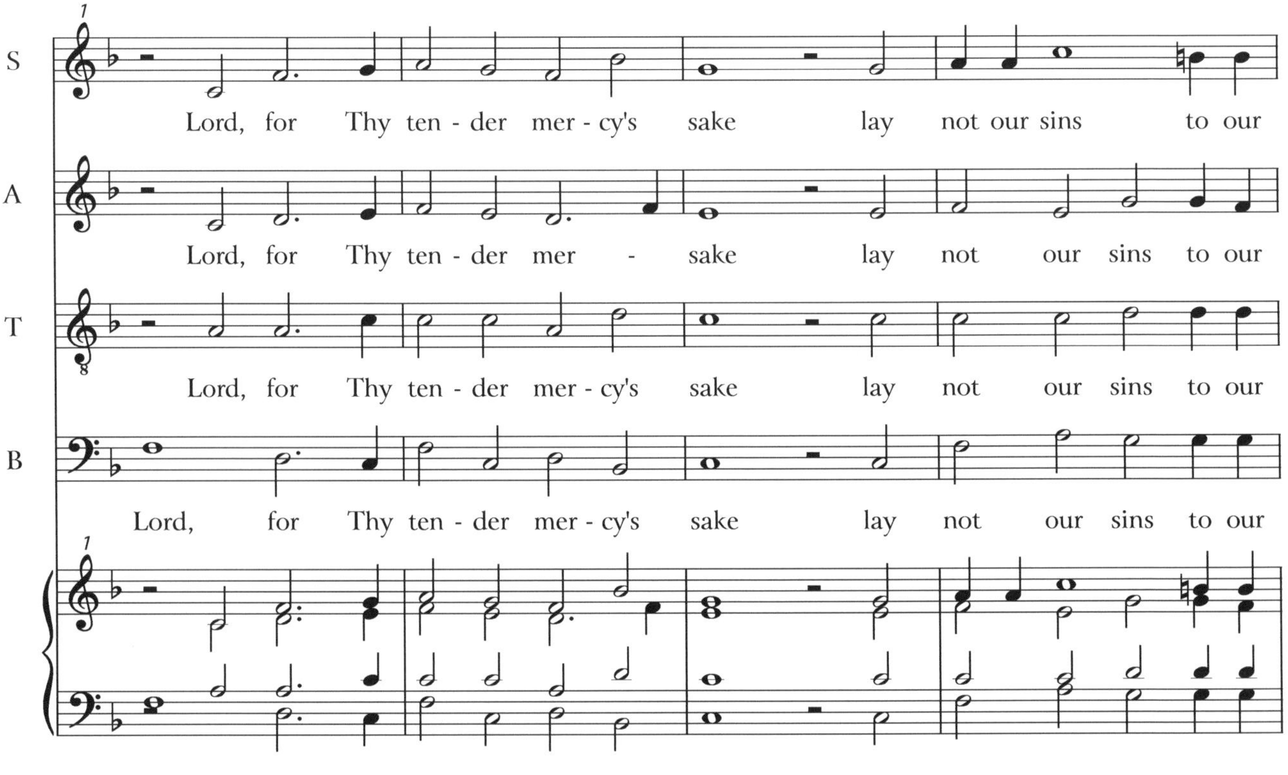

1
S
Lord, for Thy ten - der mer - cy's sake lay not our sins to our
A
Lord, for Thy ten - der mer - sake lay not our sins to our
T
Lord, for Thy ten - der mer - cy's sake lay not our sins to our
B
Lord, for Thy ten - der mer - cy's sake lay not our sins to our
1

 copying & sharing of this music is permitted under creative commons 3.0

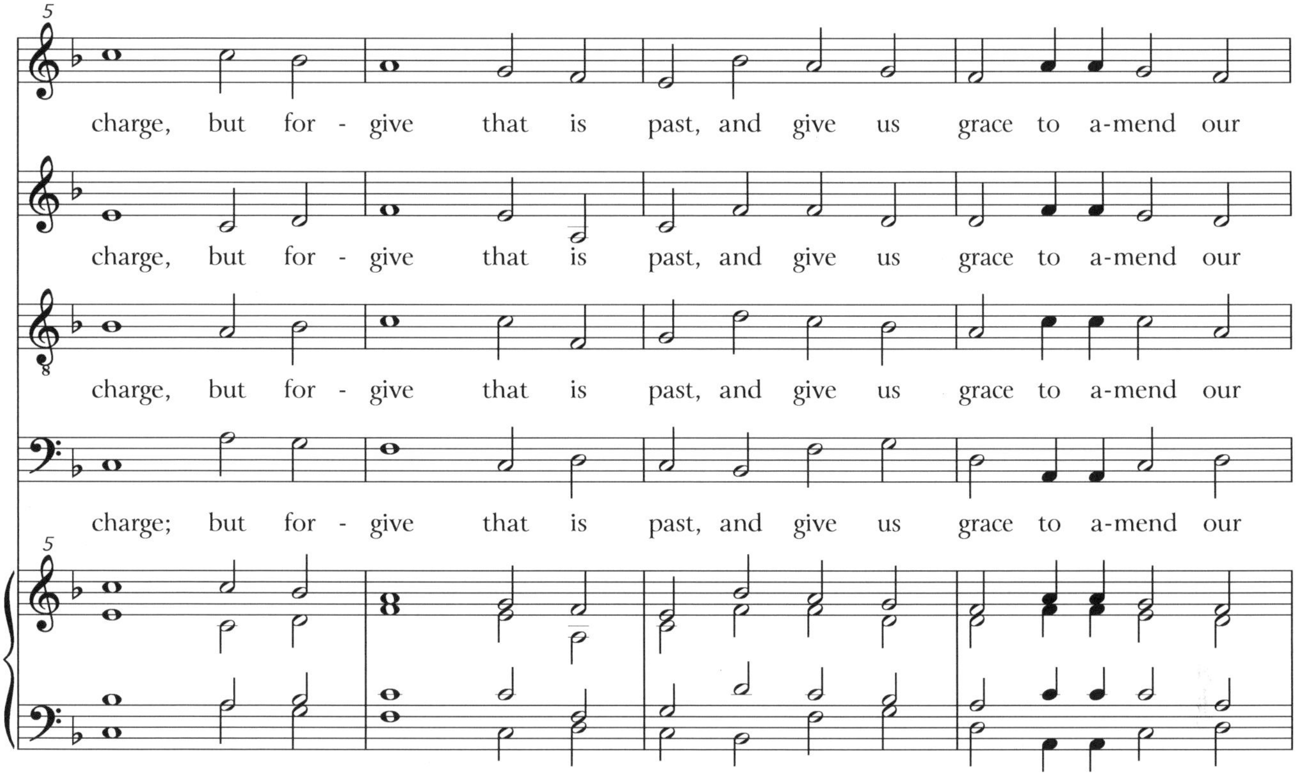

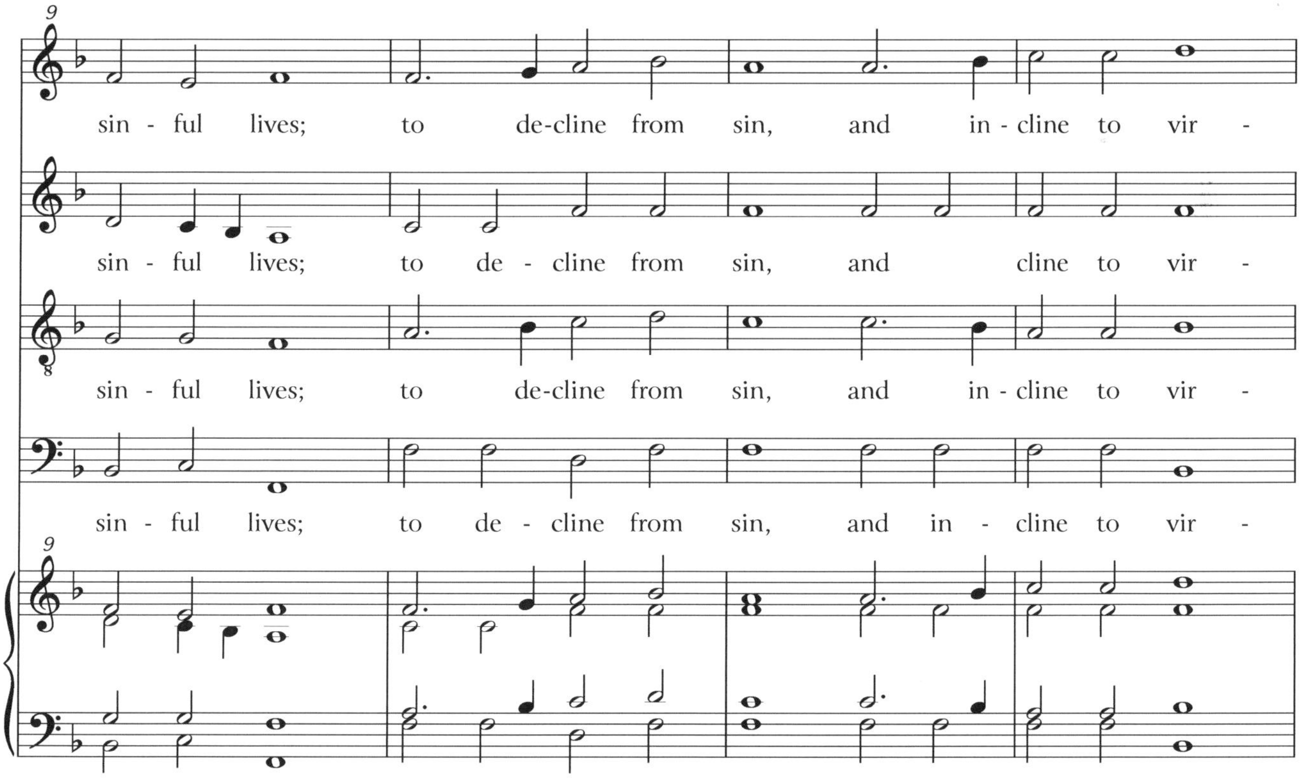

copying & sharing of this music is permitted under creative commons 3.0 • the anthology I • www.thecatholicchoirbook.com

 copying & sharing of this music is permitted under creative commons 3.0

copying & sharing of this music is permitted under creative commons 3.0 • the anthology I • www.thecatholicchoirbook.com

MISERERE MEI

Domine Non Sum Dignus

Have mercy on me, for I am weak;
heal me, O Lord, and I shall be healed.

Tomás Luis de Victoria
1548-1611

 copying & sharing of this music is permitted under creative commons 3.0

copying & sharing of this music is permitted under creative commons 3.0 • the anthology I • www.thecatholicchoirbook.com

 copying & sharing of this music is permitted under creative commons 3.0

MISERERE MEI

From Domine Non Sum Dignus

Have mercy on me, for I am weak;
heal me, O Lord, and I shall be healed.

Antonio Lotti
1667-1740

copying & sharing of this music is permitted under creative commons 3.0 • the anthology I • www.thecatholicchoirbook.com

 copying & sharing of this music is permitted under creative commons 3.0

copying & sharing of this music is permitted under creative commons 3.0 • the anthology I • www.thecatholicchoirbook.com

NON NOBIS DOMINE

Psalm 133:9

Not to us, not to us, O Lord,
But to your name give glory.

Philip van Wilder
1520-1554
Formerly thought to be by William Byrd

 copying & sharing of this music is permitted under creative commons 3.0

copying & sharing of this music is permitted under creative commons 3.0

 copying & sharing of this music is permitted under creative commons 3.0

O BONE JESU

Anon.

O good Jesus,
O most sweet Jesus,
O most pious Jesus,
O Jesus, O Jesus, O Jesus!
Have mercy on us, have mercy on us!

Michelangelo Grancini
1605-1668

S
O bo - ne Je - su, O dul - cis - si - me Je - su, O pi - is - si - me
A
O bo - ne Je - su, O dul - cis - si - me Je - su, O pi - is - si - me
B
O bo - ne Je - su, O dul - cis - si - me Je - su, O pi - is - si - me

copying & sharing of this music is permitted under creative commons 3.0 • the anthology I • www.thecatholicchoirbook.com

 copying & sharing of this music is permitted under creative commons 3.0

O BONE JESU

Trans: William Mahrt

O good Jesus, have mercy upon us, for thou hast created us, thou hast redeemed us by thy most precious blood.

Marc'Antonio Ingegneri
1547-1592
Once attributed to Palestrina

copying & sharing of this music is permitted under creative commons 3.0 • the anthology I • www.thecatholicchoirbook.com

 copying & sharing of this music is permitted under creative commons 3.0

O MAGNUM MYSTERIUM

Pedro de Cristo
c.1545-1618

O great mystery and wondrous sacrament,
that the animals should witness
the birth of the Lord in the manger.
Hail, Mary, full of grace, the Lord is with you.
Blessed are you, O Virgin, whose womb was deemed worthy
to bear the Lord Jesus Christ.

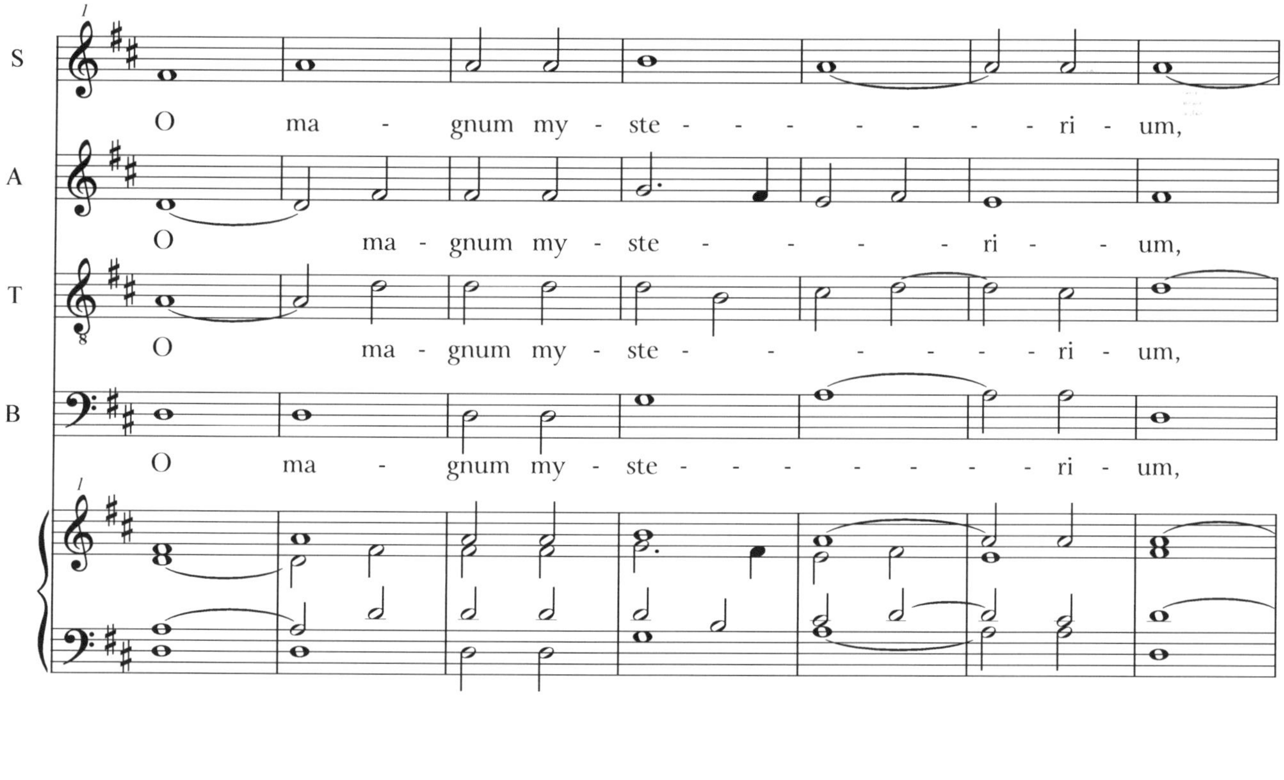

copying & sharing of this music is permitted under creative commons 3.0 • the anthology I • www.thecatholicchoirbook.com

 copying & sharing of this music is permitted under creative commons 3.0

22
ut a-ni-ma-li-a, ut a-ni-ma- - - li - - a vi-
a, ut a-ni-ma-li - a, ut a - na-ma-li - a vi-
ma-li-a, ut a-ni-ma- - - - - - - li - a vi - de-rent,
a-ni-ma-li - a, ut a-ni-ma- - - - - li - - a vi - de-rent,
22
29
de - rent, vi - de - rent Do - mi-num na - tum, ja - cen - tem in
de - rent, vi - de - rent Do - mi-num na - tum, ja - cen - tem in
vi - de - rent Do - mi-num na - tum, ja - cen - tem in
vi - de - rent Do - mi-num na - tum, ja - cen - tem in
29

 copying & sharing of this music is permitted under creative commons 3.0

50
- - - runt por - ta - re Do - mi - - -
- - runt por - ta - re Do - mi - - -
- - - runt por - ta - re Do - mi - num Chri - - - - - -
- - runt por - ta - re Do - mi - num Chri - - - -
50
57
- - num Chri - - - - - - stum.
num Chri - - - - - stum. A - - - ve Ma -
- - - - - stum.
- - - - - - - stum. A - ve Ma - ri - -
57

 copying & sharing of this music is permitted under creative commons 3.0

copying & sharing of this music is permitted under creative commons 3.0

93
por - ta - re Do - mi - - - num Chri - - - - - - stum.
por - ta - re Do - mi - num Chri - - stum.
Do - mi - num Chri - - - - - - - - - - - stum.
Do - mi - num Chri - - - - - - - stum.
93

 copying & sharing of this music is permitted under creative commons 3.0

O MAGNUM MYSTERIUM

Christmas Matins

Tomás Luis de Victoria
1548-1611

O great mystery and wondrous sacrament,
that the animals should witness the birth of the Lord in the manger.
Hail, Mary, full of grace, the Lord is with you.
Blessed are you, O Virgin,
whose womb was deemed worthy to bear the Lord Jesus Christ.

copying & sharing of this music is permitted under creative commons 3.0 • the anthology I • www.thecatholicchoirbook.com

 copying & sharing of this music is permitted under creative commons 3.0

copying & sharing of this music is permitted under creative commons 3.0 • the anthology I • www.thecatholicchoirbook.com

 copying & sharing of this music is permitted under creative commons 3.0

copying & sharing of this music is permitted under creative commons 3.0 • the anthology I • www.thecatholicchoirbook.com

www.thecatholicchoirbook.com • the anthology | copying & sharing of this music is permitted under creative commons 3.0

copying & sharing of this music is permitted under creative commons 3.0 • the anthology I • www.thecatholicchoirbook.com

 copying & sharing of this music is permitted under creative commons 3.0

O SACRUM CONVIVIUM

St. Thomas Aquinas
William Mahrt, Translation

O sacred banquet, wherein Christ is received;
the memorial of his passion is renewed;
the soul is filled with grace;
and a pledge of future glory is given to us.

Edward D'Evry
1869-1950

 copying & sharing of this music is permitted under creative commons 3.0

mf
cres.
f
mens im-ple - tur gra - ti - a: et fu - tu - rae glo - ri ae
mens im-ple - tur gra - ti - a: et fu - tu - rae glo - ri - ae
mens im-ple - tur gra - ti - a: et fu - tu - rae glo - ri - ae
mens im-ple - tur gra - ti - a: et fu - tu - rae glo - ri ae
rit.
ff
pp
a tempo
no - bis pi - ngus da - - tir. O sa - crum con -
no - bis pi - ngus da - - tur O sa - crum con -
no - bis pi - gnus da - - tur O sa - crum con -
no - bis pig - nus da - - tur O sa - crum con -

copying & sharing of this music is permitted under creative commons 3.0 • the anthology I • www.thecatholicchoirbook.com

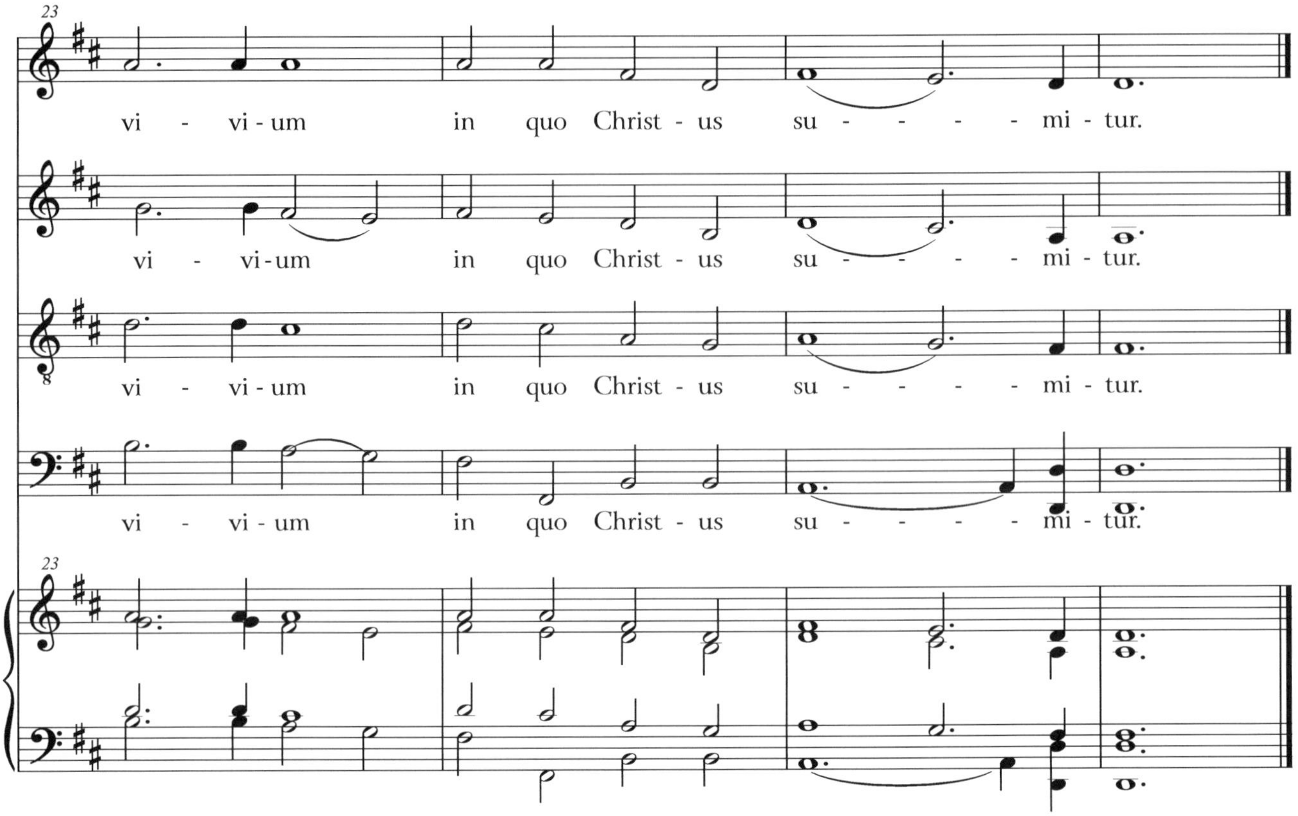
23
vi - vi - um in quo Christ - us su - - - - mi - tur.
vi - vi-um in quo Christ - us su - - - - mi - tur.
vi - vi - um in quo Christ - us su - - - - mi - tur.
vi - vi - um in quo Christ - us su - - - - mi - tur.
23

 copying & sharing of this music is permitted under creative commons 3.0

O SACRUM CONVIVIUM

St. Thomas Aquinas
1225-1274
William Mahrt, Translation

O sacred banquet, wherein Christ is received;
the memorial of his passion is renewed;
the soul is filled with grace;
and a pledge of future glory is given to us.

Roberto Remondi
1851-1928

1
S
O sa - crum con - vi - vi-um! in quo Chris - tus su - mi-tur: re -
A
O sa - crum con - vi - vi-um! in quo Chris - tus su - mi-tur: re -
T
O sa - crum con - vi - vi-um! in quo Chris - tus su - mi-tur: re -
B
O sa - crum con - vi - vi-um! in quo Chris - tus su - mi-tur: re -
1

copying & sharing of this music is permitted under creative commons 3.0 • the anthology I • www.thecatholicchoirbook.com

 copying & sharing of this music is permitted under creative commons 3.0

copying & sharing of this music is permitted under creative commons 3.0 • the anthology I • www.thecatholicchoirbook.com

PANIS ANGELICUS

St. Thomas Aquinas
1225-1274

Fr. Louis Lambillotte, S.J.
1796-1855
Arr. Noel Jones

Thus Angels' Bread is made
the Bread of man today:
the Living Bread from heaven
with figures dost away:
O wondrous gift indeed!
the poor and lowly may
upon their Lord and Master feed.

Thee, therefore, we implore,
o Godhead, One in Three,
so may Thou visit us
as we now worship Thee;
and lead us on Thy way,
That we at last may see
the light wherein Thou dwellest aye.

Pa - nis an - ge - li-cus fit pa-nis ho - mi-num; Dat pa-nis coe - li-cus
Pa - nis an - ge - li-cus fit pa-nis ho - mi-num; Dat pa-nis coe - li-cus
Pa - nis an - ge - li-cus fit pa-nis ho - mi-num; Dat pa-nis coe - li-cus
Pa - nis an - ge - li-cus fit pa-nis ho - mi-num; Dat pa-nis coe - li-cus

 copying & sharing of this music is permitted under creative commons 3.0

11
fi - gu - ris ter - mi - num: O res mi - ra - bi - lis! man - du - cat
fi - gu - ris ter - mi - num: O res mi - ra - bi - lis! man - du - cat
fi - gu - ris ter - mi - num: O res mi - ra - bi - lis! man - du - cat
ter - mi - num; O res mi - ra - bi - lis! man - du - cat
11
17
Do - mi - num Pau - per, ser - vus, et hu - mi - lis.
Do - mi - num Pau - per, ser - vus, et hu - mi - lis.
Do - mi - num Pau - per, ser - vus, et hu - mi - lis.
Do - mi - num Pau - per, ser - vus, et hu - mi - lis.
17

 copying & sharing of this music is permitted under creative commons 3.0

36
co - li - mus; Per tu - as se - mi - tas duc nos quo ten - di - mus,
co - li - mus; Per tu - as se - mi - tas duc nos quo ten - di - mus,
co - li - mus; Per tu - as se - mi - tas duc nos quo ten - di - mus,
co - li - mus; Per tu - as se - mi - tas duc nos quo ten - di - mus,
36
42
Ad lu - cem quam in - ha - - bi - tas.
Ad lu - cem quam in - ha - - bi - tas.
Ad lu - cem quam in - ha - - bi - tas.
Ad lu - cem quam in - ha - - bi - tas.
42

copying & sharing of this music is permitted under creative commons 3.0 • the anthology I • www.thecatholicchoirbook.com

PRAYER OF KING HENRY VI

King Henry VI
1422-1461

Henry G. Ley
1887-1962

Lord Jesus Christ,
who created,redeemed, and preordained me
to be this that I am, you know what you wish to do
with me;
do with me in accordance
with your will, with mercy.
Amen.

 copying & sharing of this music is permitted under creative commons 3.0

copying & sharing of this music is permitted under creative commons 3.0 • the anthology I • www.thecatholicchoirbook.com

 copying & sharing of this music is permitted under creative commons 3.0

REMEMBER, REMEMBER NOT

1789 Book Of Common Prayer

Henry Purcell
1659-1695

copying & sharing of this music is permitted under creative commons 3.0 • the anthology I • www.thecatholicchoirbook.com

www.thecatholicchoirbook.com • the anthology | copying & sharing of this music is permitted under creative commons 3.0

23
Lord, nei - - - ther take thou ven - geance of our sins but spare
of our sins, nei - - - ther take thou ven - geance of our
nei - ther take thou ven - geance of our sins, good Lord
ven - geance of our sins, but spare us good
23
27
us good Lord, spare us good Lord, spare thy
sins but spare us good Lord, spare thy
but spare us, spare us good Lord, spare thy
Lord, but spare us good Lord, spare thy
27

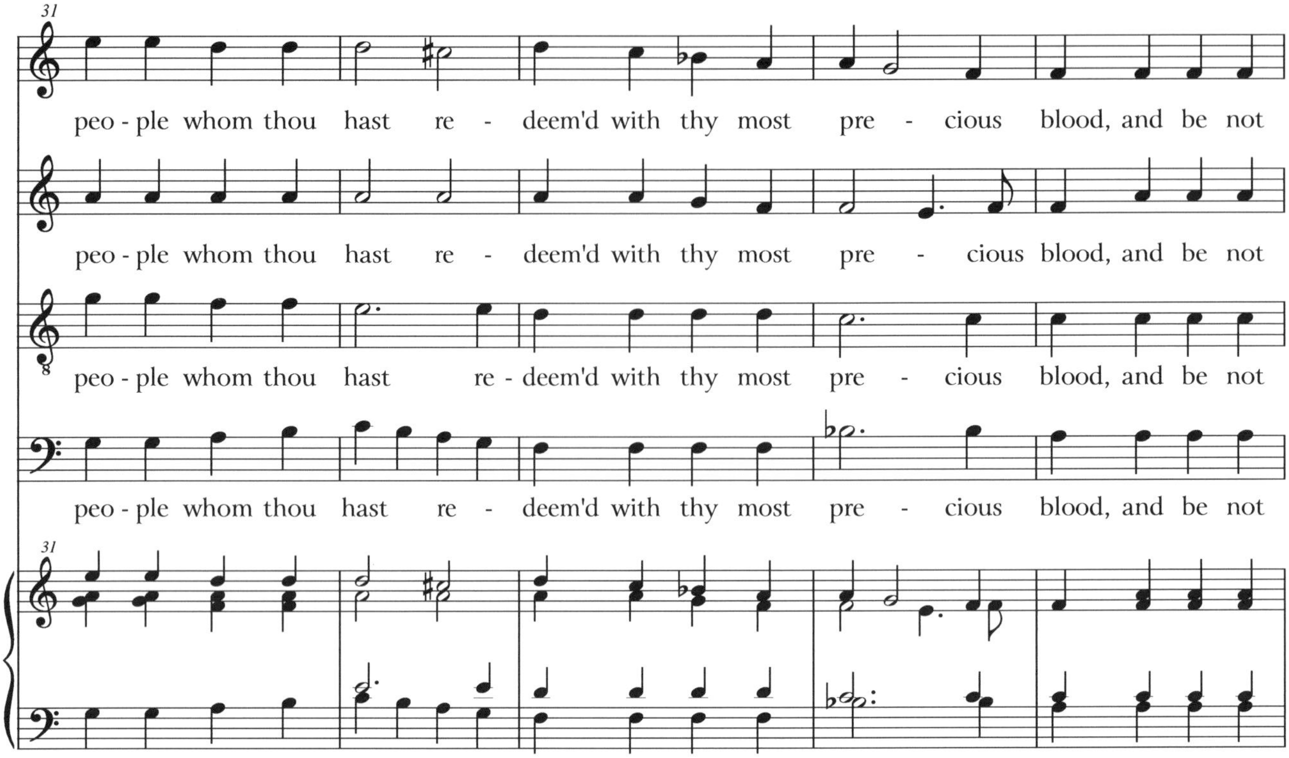

 copying & sharing of this music is permitted under creative commons 3.0

41
us for - ev - - - - er, spare us, good Lord.
us for - ev - - - - er, spare us, good Lord.
us for - ev - - - - er, spare us, good Lord.
us for - ev - - - - er, spare us, good Lord.
41

copying & sharing of this music is permitted under creative commons 3.0 • the anthology I • www.thecatholicchoirbook.com

SALVE REGINA

Hail, holy Queen, Mother of Mercy,
our life, our sweetness and our hope.
To thee do we cry, poor banished children of Eve;
to thee do we send up our sighs,
mourning and weeping in this valley of tears.
Turn then, most gracious advocate,
thine eyes of mercy toward us;
and after this our exile,
show unto us the blessed fruit of thy womb, Jesus.
O clement, O loving, O sweet Virgin Mary.

Sigismund Ritter von Neukomm
1778-1858

Andante

www.thecatholicchoirbook.com • the anthology | copying & sharing of this music is permitted under creative commons 3.0

6
ce - - do et spes nost - rae sal - ve. Ad te cla - ma - mus
ce - - do et spes nost - rae sal - ve. Ad te cla - ma - mus
et spes nost - rae sal - ve. Ad te cla - ma - mus

11
ex - su-les fi - li - i E - vae, ad Te sus - pi - ra - mus ge-men - tes et
ex - su-les fi - li - i E - vae, ad Te sus - pi - ra - mus ge-men - tes et
ex - su-les fi - li - i E - vae, ad Te sus - pi - ra - mus ge-men - tes et

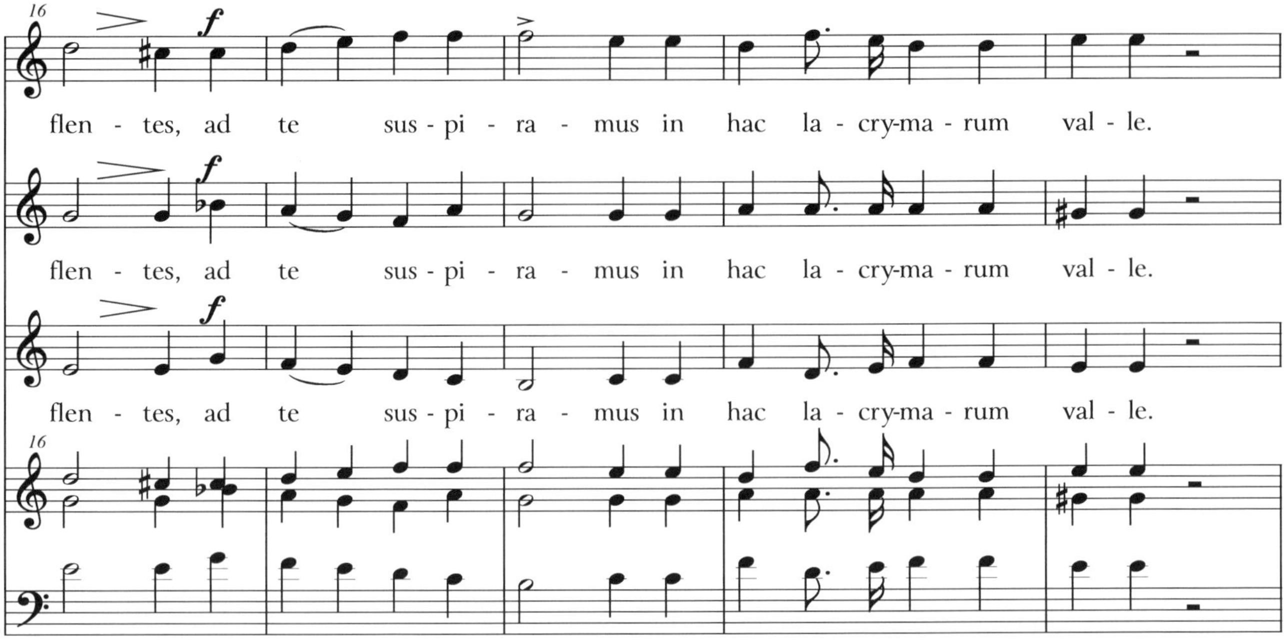
16
f
flen - tes, ad te sus - pi - ra - mus in hac la - cry-ma - rum val - le.
f
flen - tes, ad te sus - pi - ra - mus in hac la - cry-ma - rum val - le.
f
flen - tes, ad te sus - pi - ra - mus in hac la - cry-ma - rum val - le.
16

21
p
f
p
E - ja er - go ad - vo - ca - ta nost - ra il - los
p
f
p
E - ja er - go ad - vo - ca - ta nost - ra il - los
p
f
p
E - ja er - go ad - vo - ca - ta nost - ra il - los
21

 copying & sharing of this music is permitted under creative commons 3.0

copying & sharing of this music is permitted under creative commons 3.0 • the anthology I • www.thecatholicchoirbook.com

36
fruc - tum vent - ris tu - - - - - i post hoc e - xi - li-um
dic - tum fruc-tum vent - - - ris tu - i post hoc e - xi - li-um
dic - tum fruc-tum vent-ris tu - - - - - i post hoc e - xi - li-um
36

41
no - bis os - ten - de. Oh cle - mens, Oh
no - bis os - ten - de. Oh cle - mens, Oh
no - bis os - ten - de. Oh cle - mens, Oh
41

www.thecatholicchoirbook.com • the anthology I copying & sharing of this music is permitted under creative commons 3.0

46
p
pi - a, Oh dul - cis vir - go Ma - ri - - - - - a, Oh cle - mens,
p
pi - a, Oh dul - cis vir - go Ma - ri - - - - - a, Oh
p
pi - a, Oh dul - cis vir - go Ma - ri - - - - - a, Oh
46

51
Oh pi - a, Oh dul - cis vir - go Ma - ri - - - - - a.
cle - mens, Oh pi - a, Oh dul - cis vir - go Ma - ri - - - - - a.
cle - mens, Oh pi - a, Oh dul - cis vir - go Ma - ri - - - - - a.
51

STABAT MATER

Sorrowful, weeping stood the Mother
by the cross on which hung her Son.

Giovanni Battista Pergolesi
1710-1736

 copying & sharing of this music is permitted under creative commons 3.0

copying & sharing of this music is permitted under creative commons 3.0 • the anthology I • www.thecatholicchoirbook.com

de - - - bat fi - li-us. Sta -
pen - de - bat fi - li - us.
25
bat ma - - - ter do - - - lo - ro - - - - - sa
Sta - - - bat ma - - - ter do - - - lo - ro - sa
29
jux - ta cru - cem la - cri - mo - - - - - - - -
jux - ta cru - cem, jux - ta cru - cem la - cri - mo - - - - - - -
33

 copying & sharing of this music is permitted under creative commons 3.0

tr
sa, dum pen-de-bat, dum pen-de - bat fi - li-us,
sa, dum pen-de-bat, dum pen-de - bat fi - li us,
37
do - lo-ro-sa, dum pen - de - bat
la - cri-mo-sa, dum pen - de - - - bat
41
fi - li-us.
fi - li-us.
45

copying & sharing of this music is permitted under creative commons 3.0 • the anthology I • www.thecatholicchoirbook.com

TANTUM ERGO

Last Verses of Pange Lingua
St. Thomas Aquinas
1225-1274

Down in adoration falling,
Lo! the sacred Host we hail,
Lo! o'er ancient forms departing
Newer rites of grace prevail;
Faith for all defects supplying,
Where the feeble senses fail.

To the everlasting Father,
And the Son Who reigns on high
With the Holy Ghost proceeding
Forth from Each eternally,
Be salvation, honor, blessing,
Might and endless majesty. Amen.

Kevin Allen
1965

Kevin Allen's Website: http://kevinallen.info/

© Kevin Allen • Provided here under Creative Commons 3.0,
copying and sharing permited except for commercial purposes.

copying & sharing of this music is permitted under creative commons 3.0 • the anthology I • www.thecatholicchoirbook.com

 copying & sharing of this music is permitted under creative commons 3.0

copying & sharing of this music is permitted under creative commons 3.0 • the anthology I • www.thecatholicchoirbook.com

 copying & sharing of this music is permitted under creative commons 3.0

copying & sharing of this music is permitted under creative commons 3.0 • the anthology I • www.thecatholicchoirbook.com

260

TANTUM ERGO

St. Thomas Aquinas
1225-1274

Giovanni Pierluigi da Palestrina
1525-1594

Down in adoration falling,
Lo! the sacred Host we hail,
Lo! oe'r ancient forms departing
Newer rites of grace prevail;
Faith for all defects supplying,
Where the feeble senses fail.

To the everlasting Father,
And the Son Who reigns on high
With the Holy Spirit proceeding
Forth from each eternally,
Be salvation, honor blessing,
Might and endless majesty.
Amen.

www.thecatholicchoirbook.com • the anthology I copying & sharing of this music is permitted under creative commons 3.0

copying & sharing of this music is permitted under creative commons 3.0

 copying & sharing of this music is permitted under creative commons 3.0

37
stet fi - des sup - ple - men - tum Sen -
fi - des sup - ple - men - - - - - - - - -
- stet fi - - - des sup - ple - men - tum
fi - des sup - ple - men - tum sup - ple-men - - -
37
44
- - su - um de fec tu - i.
tum, Sen - - - - su - um de - -
Sen - - - - - su-um de - fec - - - - - - -
tum. Sen - - - - - su um de - - fec - - - - - -
44

 copying & sharing of this music is permitted under creative commons 3.0

copying & sharing of this music is permitted under creative commons 3.0 • the anthology I • www.thecatholicchoirbook.com

TANTUM ERGO

Last Verses of Pange Lingua
St. Thomas Aquinas
1225-1274

Déodat de Sévrác
1872-1921

Down in adoration falling,
Lo! the sacred Host we hail,
Lo! o'er ancient forms departing
Newer rites of grace prevail;
Faith for all defects supplying,
Where the feeble senses fail.

To the everlasting Father,
And the Son Who reigns on high
With the Holy Ghost proceeding
Forth from Each eternally,
Be salvation, honor, blessing,
Might and endless majesty.
Amen.

 copying & sharing of this music is permitted under creative commons 3.0

copying & sharing of this music is permitted under creative commons 3.0 • the anthology I • www.thecatholicchoirbook.com

 copying & sharing of this music is permitted under creative commons 3.0

THOU KNOWEST LORD

The Burial Service
Book of Common Prayer

Henry Purcell
1659-1695

1
S
Thou know - est, Lord, the se - crets of our hearts;
A
Thou know - est, Lord, the se - crets of our hearts;
T
Thou know - est, Lord, the se - crets of our hearts;
B
Thou know - est, Lord, the se - crets of our hearts;
1

copying & sharing of this music is permitted under creative commons 3.0 • the anthology I • www.thecatholicchoirbook.com

 copying & sharing of this music is permitted under creative commons 3.0

copying & sharing of this music is permitted under creative commons 3.0 • the anthology I • www.thecatholicchoirbook.com

 copying & sharing of this music is permitted under creative commons 3.0

S.PETRVS
S.PAVLVS

KYRIE ELEISON

Holy Mass

Lord have mercy on us,
Christ have mercy on us,
Lord have mercy on us.

William Byrd
1540-1623

 copying & sharing of this music is permitted under creative commons 3.0

GLORIA

Holy Mass

William Byrd
1540-1623

Glory to God in the highest,
and on earth peace to people of good will.
We praise you, we bless you, we adore you, we glorify you,
we give you thanks for your great glory,
Lord God, heavenly King, O God, almighty Father.
Lord Jesus Christ, Only-begotten Son, Lord God,
Lamb of God, Son of the Father,
you take away the sins of the world, have mercy on us;
you take away the sins of the world, receive our prayer.
you are seated at the right hand of the Father, have mercy on us.
For you alone are the Holy One, you alone are the Lord,
you alone are the Most High, Jesus Christ,
with the Holy Spirit, in the glory of God the Father.
Amen

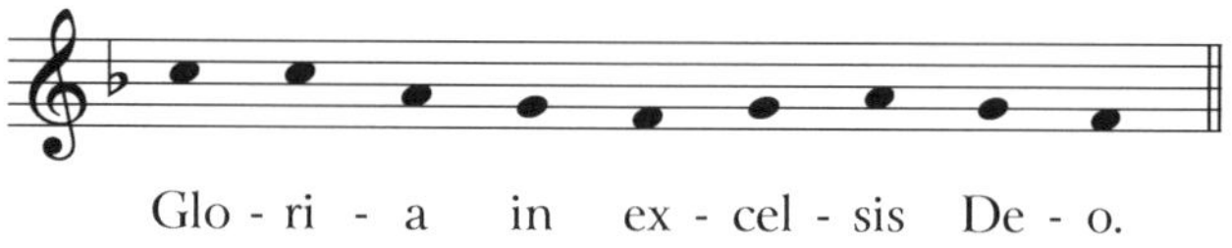

copying & sharing of this music is permitted under creative commons 3.0 • the anthology I • www.thecatholicchoirbook.com

 copying & sharing of this music is permitted under creative commons 3.0

17
mus te. Gra - ti-as a - gi-mus ti - bi pro-pter ma-gnam glo - ri-
- mus te. Gra - ti-as a - gi-mus ti - bi pro - pter ma-
ca-mus te. Gra - ti-as a - gi-mus ti - bi pro-pter ma-gnam glo-ri -
17
22
am tu - - - - am, Do - mi-ne De - us, rex cæ - le -
- gnam glo - ri - am tu - - - am, Do - mi-ne De - us,
am tu - am, Do - mi-ne De - us, rex cæ - le -
22

 copying & sharing of this music is permitted under creative commons 3.0

copying & sharing of this music is permitted under creative commons 3.0 • the anthology I • www.thecatholicchoirbook.com

48
Qui tol - lis pec-ca - ta mun -
fi - li-us pa - - - - - tris. Qui tol - lis pec-
De - i, fi - li-us pa - tris. Qui tol - lis pec - ca -
48

53
di, mi - se - re - re no - bis, mi - se - re - re no-
ca - ta mun - di, mi - se - re - re no - bis, no -
ta mu - - - di, mi - se - re - re no - bis, mi - se - re - re
53

 copying & sharing of this music is permitted under creative commons 3.0

58
- - bis, Qui tol - lis pec - ca - ta mun - di, sus - ci-pe
- - bis, Qui tol - lis pec - ca - ta mun - di, sus - ci-pe de - pre -
no - bis, Qui tol - lis pec - ca - ta mun - di,
58

63
de - pre - ca - ti - o - nem no-stram, sus - ci-pe de - pre-ca - ti - o - nem no -
ca - ti-o - nem no - stram, sus - ci-pe de - pre - ca - ti - o - nem no -
sus - ci-pe de - pre - ca - ti - o - nem no - stram, de - pre - ca - ti - o - nem
63

 copying & sharing of this music is permitted under creative commons 3.0

78
Quo - ni - am tu so - lus san - ctus, tu so - lus Do - mi - nus, tu
Quo - ni - am tu so - lus san - ctus, tu so - lus Do - mi - nus, Do - mi -
Quo - ni - am tu so - lus san - ctus, tu so - lus Do - mi-
78

83
so - lus Do - mi - nus, tu so - lus al - tis - si - - - mus, tu
nus, tu so - lus Do - mi - nus, tu so - lus al - tis - si - mus, tu
nus, tu so - lus al - tis - si - mus, tu so - lus al - tis -
83

copying & sharing of this music is permitted under creative commons 3.0 • the anthology I • www.thecatholicchoirbook.com

88
so - lus al - tis - si - mus, Je - su Chri - ste, cum san - cto
so - lus al - tis - si - mus, Je - su Chri - ste, cum san - cto Spi - ri -
- si - mus, Je - su Chri - ste, cum san - cto Spi - ri - tu, cum
88

93
Spi - ri - tu, in glo - ri - a De - i pa -
tu, in glo - ri - a De - i pa - - - tris,
san - cto Spi - ri - tu, Spi - ri - tu, in glo - ri - a De -
93

 copying & sharing of this music is permitted under creative commons 3.0

97
tris, in glo - ri - a De - i pa - - tris. A -
in glo - ri - a De - i pa - - - - - - tris. A - - -
- i pa - - - tris, De - i pa - - - - - - - tris. A - - -
97
102
- - men. A - - - - - - - - - men.
- - - - - men. A - - - - - - - - - men.
- - - - - - - men. A - men.
102

copying & sharing of this music is permitted under creative commons 3.0 • the anthology I • www.thecatholicchoirbook.com

CREDO

Holy Mass

I believe in God, the Father almighty, creator of heaven and earth.
I believe in Jesus Christ, his only Son, our Lord.
He was conceived by the power of the Holy Spirit
and born of the Virgin Mary.
He suffered under Pontius Pilate, was crucified, died, and was buried.
He descended to the dead. On the third day he rose again.
He ascended into heaven and is seated at the right hand of the Father.
He will come again to judge the living and the dead.
I believe in the Holy Spirit,
the holy catholic Church, the communion of saints,
the forgiveness of sins,
the resurrection of the body,
and life everlasting.
Amen.

William Byrd
1540-1623

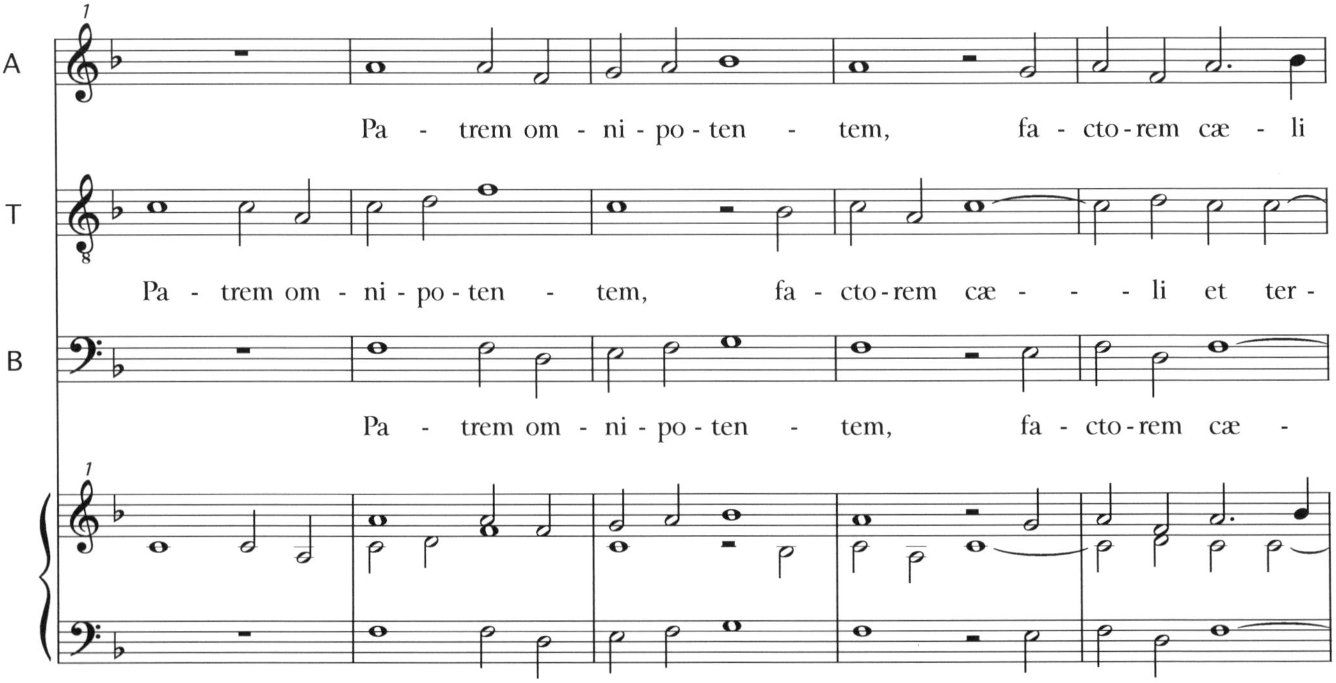

 copying & sharing of this music is permitted under creative commons 3.0

copying & sharing of this music is permitted under creative commons 3.0 • the anthology I • www.thecatholicchoirbook.com

16
um De - i u - ni - ge - ni - tum, Et ex pa - tre na -
- li-um De - i u-ni-ge - ni - tum, Et ex pa - tre na - -
um De - i u - ni - ge - ni - tum, an -
16

21
tum an - te om - ni-a sæ - cu - la, De - um de De - o,
tum, De - um de De - o, lu - men de
te om - ni - a sæ - - - cu - la, De - um de De - o,
21

 copying & sharing of this music is permitted under creative commons 3.0

copying & sharing of this music is permitted under creative commons 3.0 • the anthology I • www.thecatholicchoirbook.com

 copying & sharing of this music is permitted under creative commons 3.0

45
no - stram sa - lu - - - tem de - scen - dit, de -
et pro-pter no - stram sa - lu - - - - - tem de - scen - dit
- mi-nes, et pro-pter no - stram sa - lu - - - tem, de-scen -
45

50
scen - dit de cæ - - - - - - - - lis. Et in - car -
de cæ - - - - - - - - - - - lis. Et in - car -
dit, de cæ - - - - - - - - - lis. Et in - car -
50

copying & sharing of this music is permitted under creative commons 3.0 • the anthology I • www.thecatholicchoirbook.com

54
na - tus est de spi - ri-tu san - - - cto, ex Ma-ri -
na - tus est de spi - ri - tu san - - - cto, ex Ma - ri - a
na - tus est, de spi - ri-tu san - cto, ex Ma - ri - a
54

59
- a vir - - - gi - ne, et ho - mo fa - - - ctus est, Cru -
vir - gi - ne, et ho - mo fa - - - ctus est,
vir - gi - ne, et ho - mo fa - - - ctus est, Cru - ci - fi -
59

 copying & sharing of this music is permitted under creative commons 3.0

64
- ci - fi - xus e - ti-am pro no - bis, sub Pon - ti - o Pi -
Cru - ci - fi - xus e - ti-am pro no - bis, sub
xus e - ti-am pro no - bis sub Pon - ti - o Pi - la - to,
64

69
la - to, pa - sus et se - pul - tus est, et se - pul - tus est.
Pon - ti - o Pi - la - to pas - sus et se - pul - tus est, se - pul - tus
pas - sus et se - pul - tus est, pas - sus et se - pul - tus
69

 copying & sharing of this music is permitted under creative commons 3.0

copying & sharing of this music is permitted under creative commons 3.0 • the anthology I • www.thecatholicchoirbook.com

 copying & sharing of this music is permitted under creative commons 3.0

103
e - rit fi - nis.
rit fi - nis, fi - nis. Et in Spi - ri - tum San - ctum Do - mi-num, et
fi - - - nis. Et in Spi - ri - tum san - ctum Do - mi - num,
103

109
vi - vi - fi - can - tem, qui ex pa - tre fi - li - o - que pro - ce -
et vi - vi - fi - can - tem, qui ex pa - tre fi - li - o -
109

 copying & sharing of this music is permitted under creative commons 3.0

copying & sharing of this music is permitted under creative commons 3.0 • the anthology I • www.thecatholicchoirbook.com

 copying & sharing of this music is permitted under creative commons 3.0

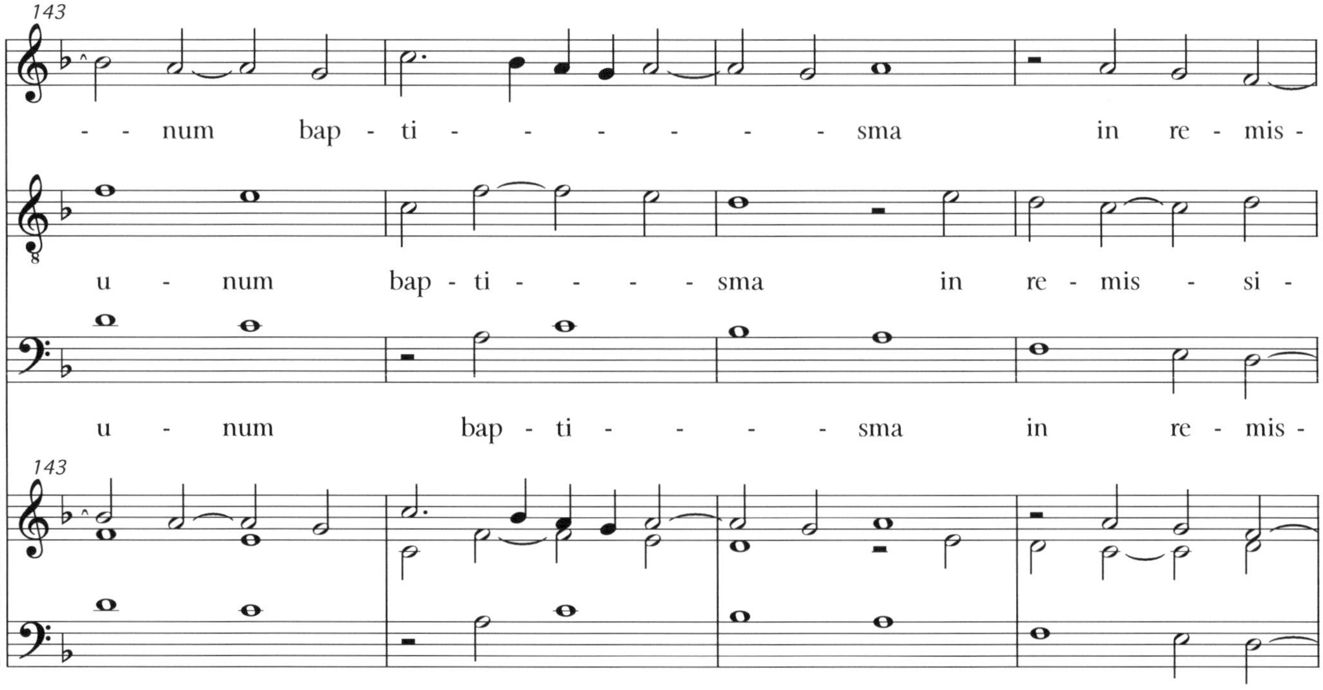

copying & sharing of this music is permitted under creative commons 3.0 • the anthology I • www.thecatholicchoirbook.com

 copying & sharing of this music is permitted under creative commons 3.0

159
et vi - tam ven-tu - - - ri sæ - cu - - - - - li.
- - cu - li, et vi - tam ven-tu - ri sæ - cu - - - li.
vi - tam ven-tu - ri sæ - - - cu - li, sæ - - - - cu - li.
159

163
A - - - - men. A - - - - - - men.
A - - - - - men. A - - - - - - - men.
A - - - - - - men. A - - - - men.
163

SANCTUS

Holy Mass

Holy, holy, holy
Lord God of Hosts.
Heaven and earth are full of your glory.
Hosanna in the highest.
Blessed is he who comes
in the name of the Lord.
Hosanna in the highest.

William Byrd
1540-1623

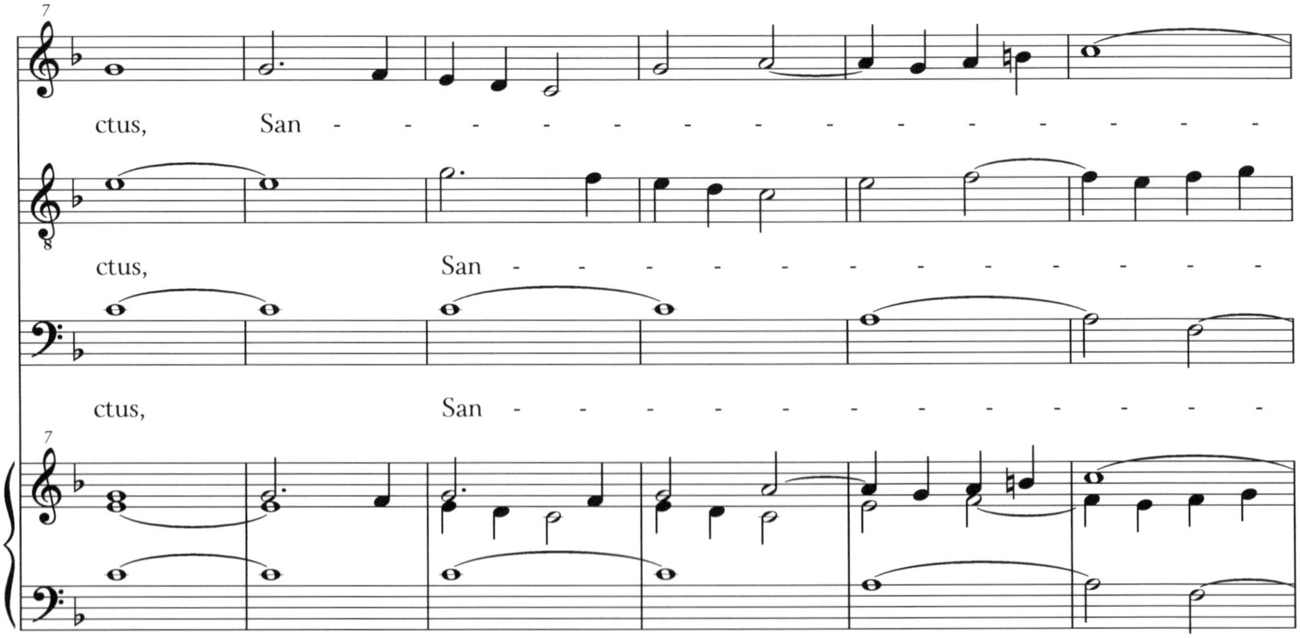

 copying & sharing of this music is permitted under creative commons 3.0

13
- - - ctus, San - - - - - - - - -
- - - - - - - ctus, San - - - - - -
- - - - - - - ctus, San - - - - - -
13

19
- - - - - - - - - - - - - - ctus, Do - mi -
- - - - - - - - - - - - - - ctus,
- - - - - - - - - - - - - - ctus.
19

25
nus De - - - - us Sa - - - ba - - - - oth, Do - mi -
Do - mi - nus De - - - - us Sa - ba - oth, Do - mi - nus
Do - mi - nus De - us Sa - ba -
25

31
nus De - - - - us Sa - - - ba - - - - oth. Ple -
De - - - - - - us Sa - - ba - oth. Ple - - -
oth, De - us Sa - - ba - oth.
31

 copying & sharing of this music is permitted under creative commons 3.0

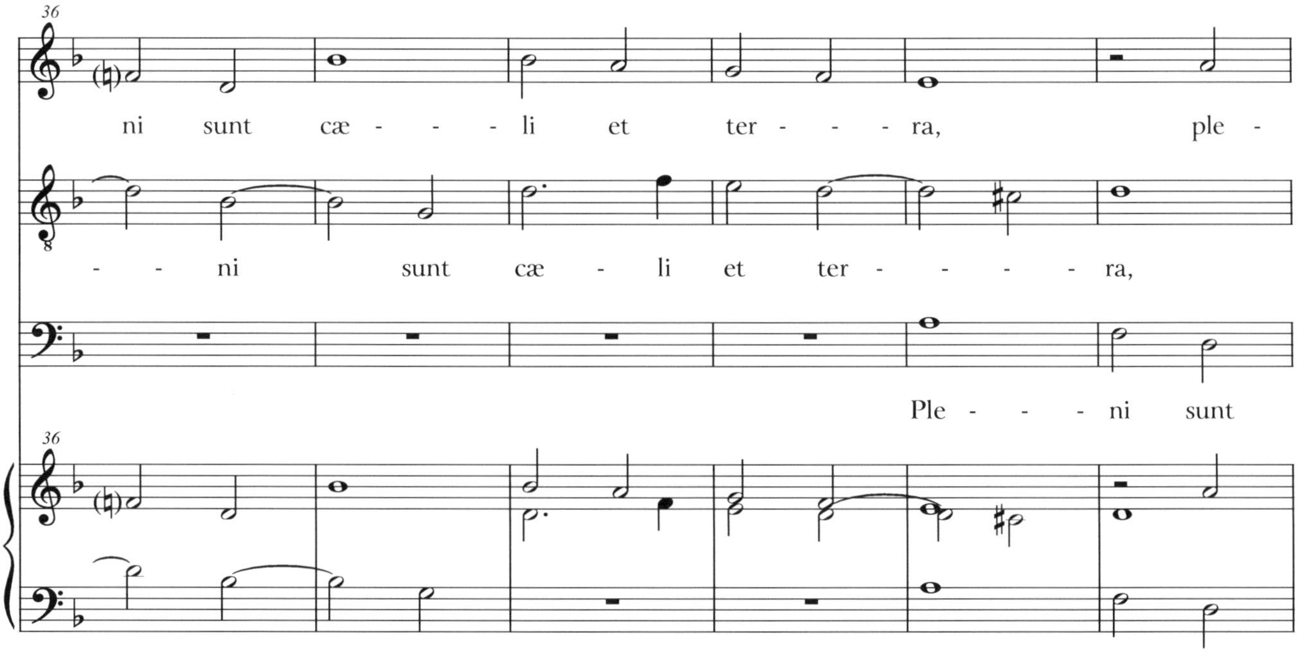

copying & sharing of this music is permitted under creative commons 3.0 • the anthology I • www.thecatholicchoirbook.com

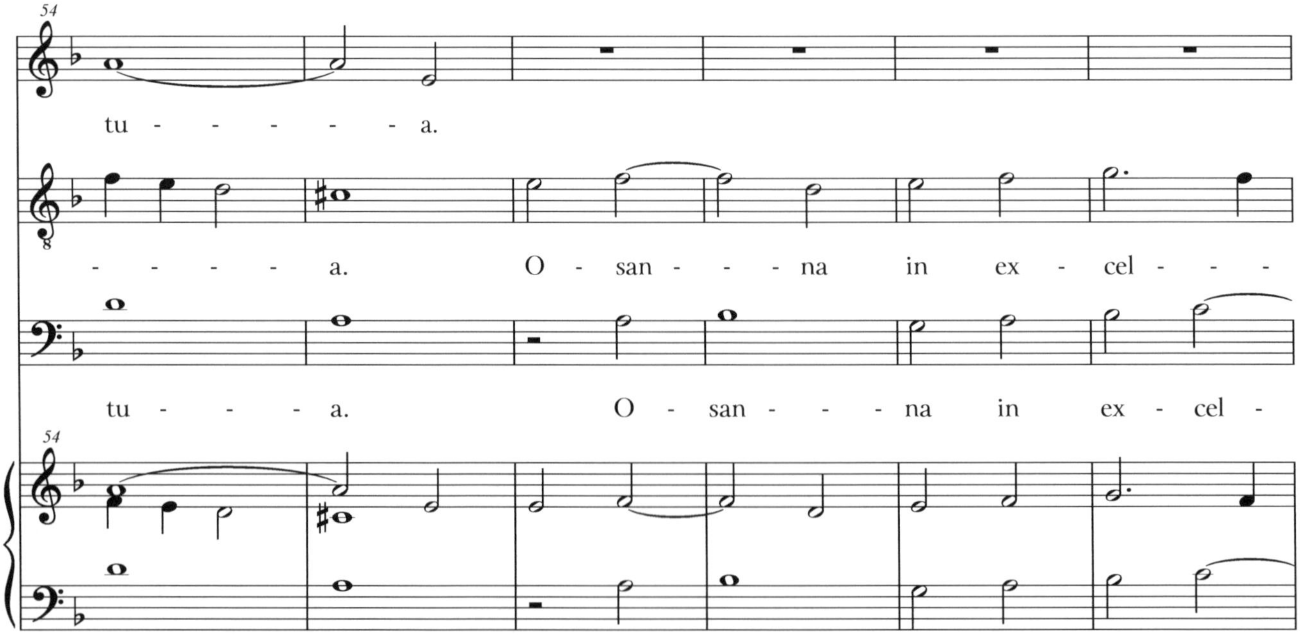

 copying & sharing of this music is permitted under creative commons 3.0

60
O - san - na in ex - cel - - - - - - - sis,
- - - - - - - - - - - - - - - - - sis, O -
- - - sis, O - san - na in ex - cel - - -
60

66
O - san - na in ex - cel - - - - - - - - -
san - na in ex - cel - - - - - - - sis, in ex -
- - - - sis, O - san - na in ex - cel - - -
66

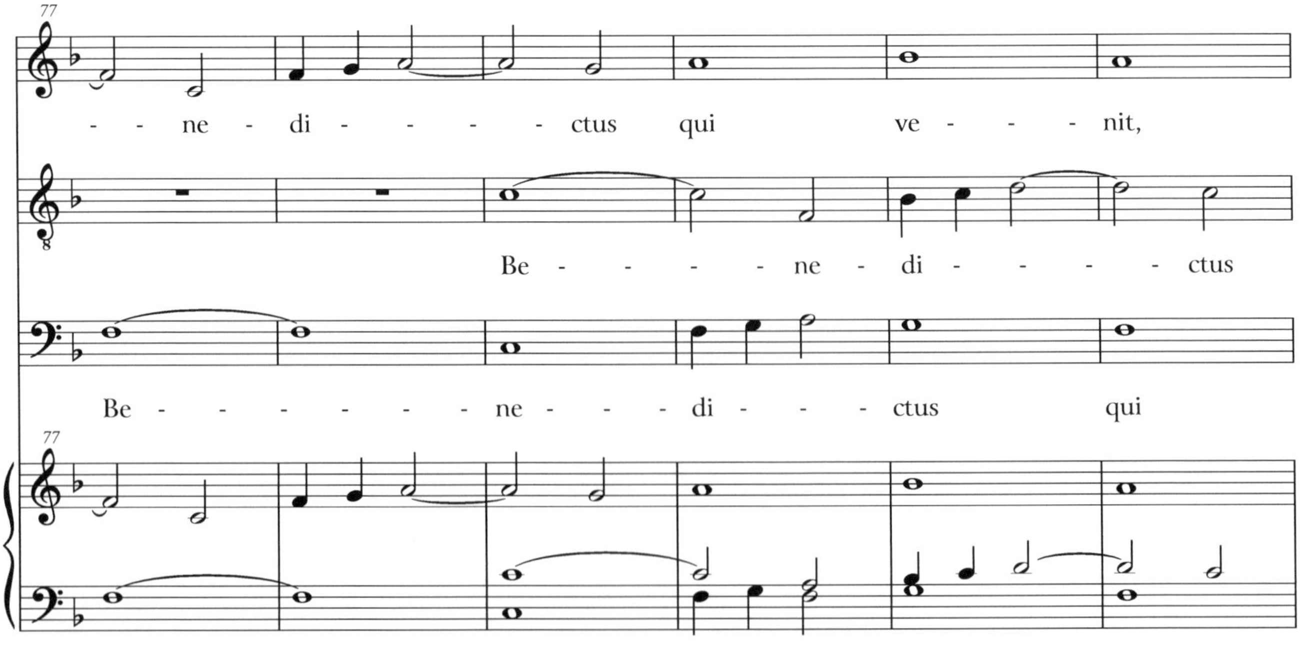

 copying & sharing of this music is permitted under creative commons 3.0

83
in no - mi - ne Do - - - mi - ni, Do - mi - ni, in
qui ve - - - - - - - - - nit, in no - mi -
ve - - - nit in no - mi - ne Do - - - - mi -
83

89
no - mi - ne Do - - - mi - ni. O - san - na
ne Do - - - - - - mi - - - - - - ni. O - san - na
ni, in no - mi - ne Do - mi - ni. O -
89

 copying & sharing of this music is permitted under creative commons 3.0

AGNUS DEI

Holy Mass

Lamb of God, you who take away the sins of the world, have mercy upon us.
Lamb of God, you who take away the sins of the world, have mercy upon us.
Lamb of God, you who take away the sins of the world, grant us peace.

William Byrd
1540-1623

copying & sharing of this music is permitted under creative commons 3.0 • the anthology I • www.thecatholicchoirbook.com

 copying & sharing of this music is permitted under creative commons 3.0

copying & sharing of this music is permitted under creative commons 3.0 • the anthology I • www.thecatholicchoirbook.com

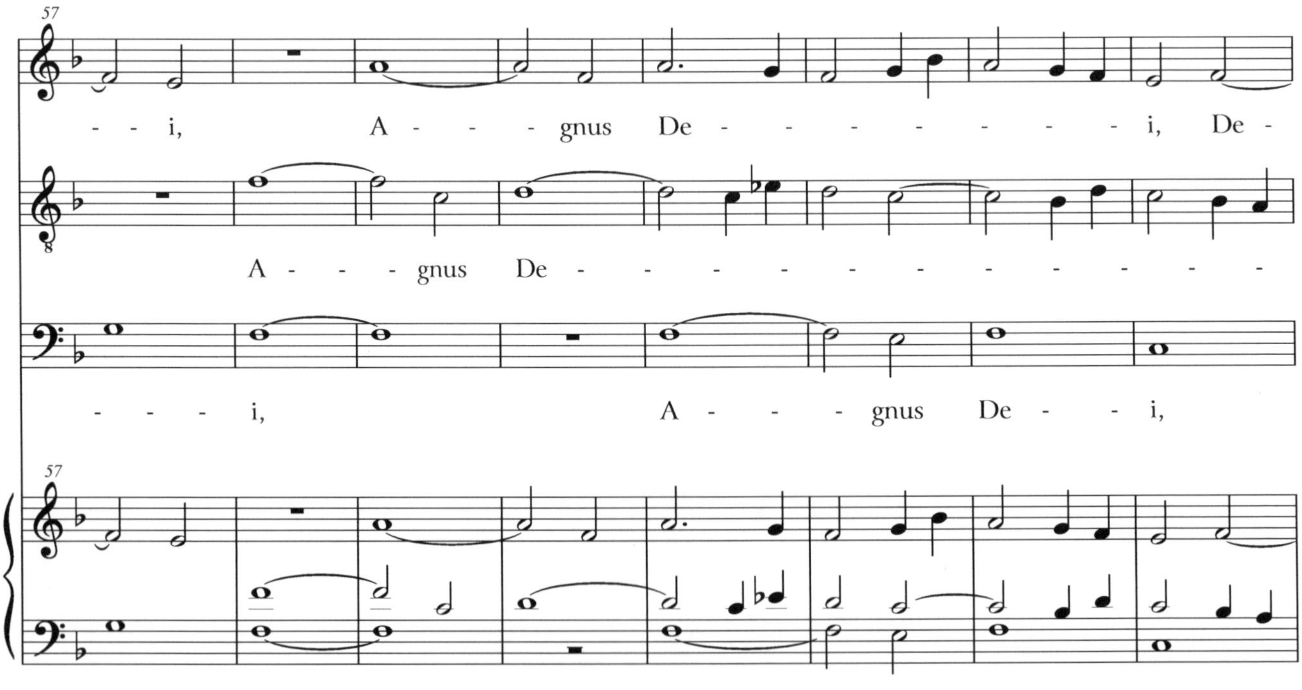

 copying & sharing of this music is permitted under creative commons 3.0

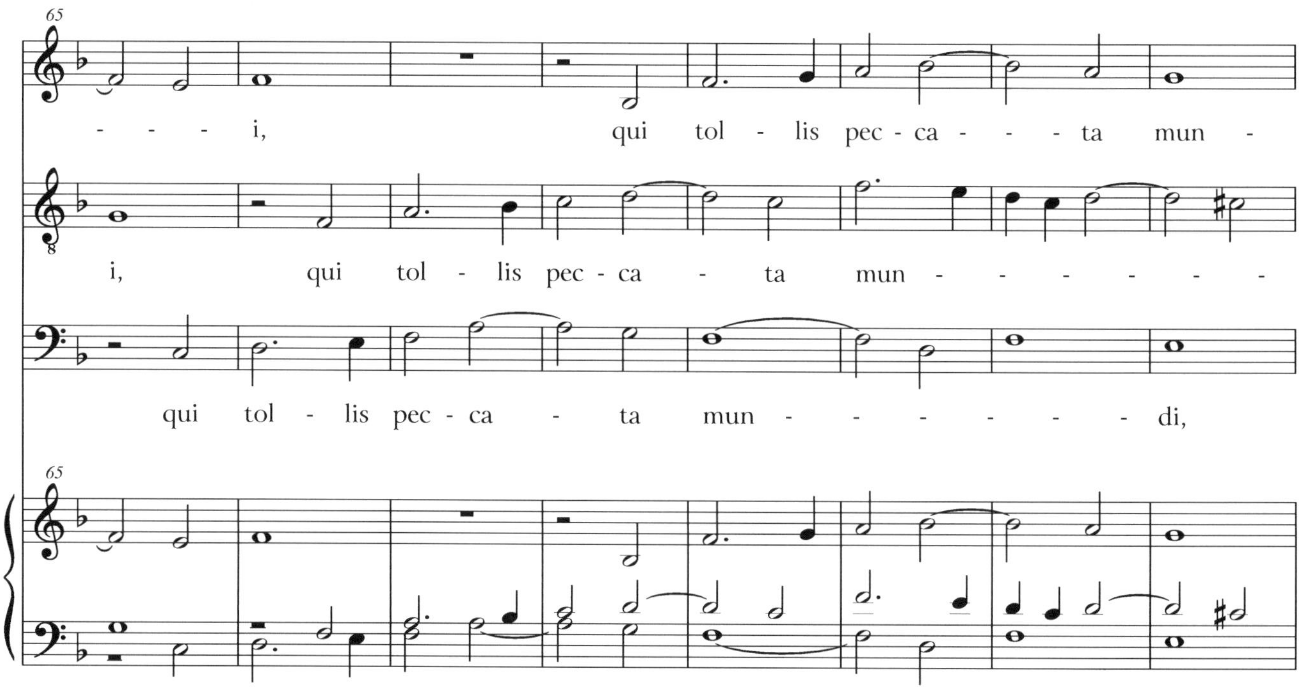

copying & sharing of this music is permitted under creative commons 3.0 • the anthology I • www.thecatholicchoirbook.com

 copying & sharing of this music is permitted under creative commons 3.0

copying & sharing of this music is permitted under creative commons 3.0 • the anthology I • www.thecatholicchoirbook.com

 copying & sharing of this music is permitted under creative commons 3.0

AND I SHALL SEE HIS FACE

OLIVE 8.6.8.6 Noel Jones
William Cowper 1731-1800

1. This is the feast of heav'-nly wine;
2. Oh, bless the Sav - iour, ye that eat,
3. The vile, the lost, He calls to them,
4. Ap - proach ye poor, nor dare re - fuse
5. If guilt and sin af - ford a plea,
And God in - vites to sup; The juic - es
With roy - al dain - ties fed; Not heav'n af -
Ye trem - bling souls ap - pear! The right - eous,
The ban - quet spread for you; Dear Sav - iour,
And may ob - tain a place; Sur - ely the
of the liv - - - - - - ing vine
fords a cost - - - - - lier treat,
in their own es - teem.
this is wel - - - - - - come news,
Lord will wel - - - - - - come me,
were pressed, to fill the cup.
for Je - - - sus is the bread.
Have no ac - cep - tance here.
That I may ven - ture too.
And I shall see His Face!

copying & sharing of this music is permitted under creative commons 3.0 • the anthology I • www.thecatholicchoirbook.com

AS THE DEWY SHADES OF EVEN

German Melody [later known as STUTTGART]
Anonymous

1. As the dew - y shades of e - ven Gath - er o'er the
2. Ho - ly Mo - ther, near me ho - ver, Free my thoughts from
3. Thins own sin - less heart was bro - ken, Sor - row's sword had
balm - y air, Lis - ten, gen - tle Queen of hea - ven,
aught de - filed, With thy wings of mer - cy co - ver,
pierced its core; Ho - ly Mo - ther, by that to - ken,
lis - ten to my ves - per pray'r.
Keep from sin thy help - less child.
Now thy pi - ty I im - plore.

 copying & sharing of this music is permitted under creative commons 3.0

BE JOYFUL MARY

REGINA CAELI 8.8 with Refrains
Regina, Caeli, Jubila - Anon 169

1. Be joy - ful, Mar - y, heav'n - ly Queen, be joy - ful,
2. The Son you bore by hea - ven's grace, be joy - ful,
3. The Lord has ris - en from the dead, be joy - ful,
4. Then pray to God, O Vir - gin fair, be joy - ful,
Mar - y! Your grief is changed to joy se - rene,
Mar - y! Did by His death our guilt e - rase,
Ma - ry! He rose in glo - ry as He said,
Mar - y! That He our souls to heav - en bear,
Al - le - lu - ia! Re - joice, re - joice, O Mar - y!
Al - le - lu - ia! Re - joice, re - joice, O Mar - y!
Al - le - lu - ia! Re - joice, re - joice, O Mar - y!
Al - le - lu - ia! Re - joice, re - joice, O Mar - y!

copying & sharing of this music is permitted under creative commons 3.0 • the anthology I • www.thecatholicchoirbook.com

BEAUTIFUL SAVIOR, MIGHTIEST

ST. RICHARD GWYN 5.6.5.6.5 Noel Jones
Vincent Uher

1. Beau - ti - ful Sav - iour, Migh - ti - est in Mer - cy,
2. Son of the Fath - er, Child of Ma - ry Moth - er,
3. All laud we bring now prais - ing our Be - lov - ed,
Light pier - cing dark - ness, Joy be - yond all sor - row,
Just Jos - eph's dear boy, Cause of Great John's leap - ing,
Christ Jes - us, Sav - iour, Vic - tor, and Re - deem - er
Woun - ded for heal - ing, Dy - ing for our
Ma - ry's De - liv' - rer, Tru - est friend to
Judge of the Liv - ing, Judge of the de -
sav - ing, Vic - tim and High Priest.
Laz' - rus True God, our High King.
par - ted, Come quick - ly, Je - sus.

 copying & sharing of this music is permitted under creative commons 3.0

BREAD OF THE WORLD I

EUCHARISTIC HYMN John S.B. Hodges
Words: St. 1 Reginald Heber • St. 1b,2,2b © CC 3.0 2009 by Vincent Uher

1. Bread of the world, in mer - cy bro - ken,
2. Oh, see thy Heart by sor - ow bro - ken,
3. E - ter - nal Word, our Lord, our Sav - iour,
4. O Lamb of God, our Friend and Bro - ther,
Wine of the soul, in mer - cy shed,
here too the tears by Ma - ry shed;
Tak - ing a - way our sin and shame,
We cry for joy to meet thee here;
by whom the words of life were spo - ken,
Blest is this Feast more than mere to - ken,
In - car - nate Love, our Hope, our Trea - sure,
Now send us out to do thee ho - nour;
and in whose death our sins are dead:
thy Bo - dy bro - ken, thy Blood red.
We worship and and a - dore Thy name.
Stay with us till thy Day ap - pear.

copying & sharing of this music is permitted under creative commons 3.0 • the anthology I • www.thecatholicchoirbook.com

BREAD OF THE WORLD II

RENDEZ A DIEU

Words: St. 1 Reginald Heber • St. 1b,2,2b © CC 3.0 2009 by Vincent Uher

1. Bread of the world, in mer - cy bro - ken, Wine of the soul, in
2. E - ter - nal Word, our Lord, our Sav - iour, Tak - ing a - way our
mer - cy shed, by whom the words of life were spo - ken,
sin and shame, In - car - nate Love, our Hope, our Trea - sure,
and in whose death our sins are dead: 1b. O, see thy Heart by
We wor - ship and a - dore Thy name. 2b. O Lamb of God, our
sor - ow bro - ken, here too the tears by Ma - ry shed; Blest is
Friend and Bro - ther, We cry for joy to meet thee here; Now send
this Feast more than mere to - ken, thy Bo - dy bro - ken, thy Blood red.
us out to do thee ho - nour; Stay with us till thy Day ap - pear.

 copying & sharing of this music is permitted under creative commons 3.0

BRIGHT TORCHES IN THE DARKEST NIGHT

TYBURN L.M. Noel Jones
Vincent Uher

1. Bright tor - ches in the dark - est night, The
2. A dim - ly burn - ing wick were we, But
3. U - nite thy saints through eve - ry age And
saints of God as lights yet shine. Lord, let our
now our faith fills with thy fire For thou art
cleansed from sin lift us a - bove, O Fath - er,
wit - ness rise with theirs, And through their
all con - sum - ing love Thy per - fect
Son, and Ho - ly Ghost, One God in
prayers give grace di - vine. A - - - - men.
will our hearts de - sire.
glo - ry, one in - love.

copying & sharing of this music is permitted under creative commons 3.0 • the anthology I • www.thecatholicchoirbook.com

328

CHRIST IS OUR HOPE WHOM WE HAVE SEEN

WALSINGHAM 87.87.87.87 Noel Jones

Vincent Uher • In Honour of Irma Moré, Foundress of Our Lady of Walsingham Institutes of Catholic Culture Studies

1. Christ is our hope whom we have seen each
2. Christ is the e - vi - dence of God, The
3. Faith hope, and love are God's own gift To
4. Praise be to Christ the_E - ter - nal Word Through -
gen - er - a - tion ri - sing. All hu - man
Love whose Name sus - tains us. Let all the
souls who seek Christ's Wis - dom. The Spi - rit
out all a - ges reign - ing O glo - rious
dreams are met in Him the sub -
na - tions of the world Re - ceive
knows this age is dim: We need
Spi - rit, Lord of Life, Re - ceive
stance of our long - ing. He is the light in
the truth: Love saved us. Love clothed in flesh in
the Mind of Je - sus. So God pours out both
our heart's thanks - giv - ing. To God Most High all

 copying & sharing of this music is permitted under creative commons 3.0

dark - est night Who calls us out with lamps a - light.
Ma - ry's womb, Love raised a - gain from out the tomb,
grace and power U - pon us all to face this hour,
glo - ry be For time and for e - ter - ni - ty
To work for God's own glo - ry.
Love cal - ling us to glo - ry.
We will make known God's glo - ry.
One God in end - less glo - ry.

copying & sharing of this music is permitted under creative commons 3.0 • the anthology I • www.thecatholicchoirbook.com

330

CHRIST MY GOD, MY FAITH DISCERNING

ENGLEWOOD 8.7.8.7 D Noel Jones
Vincent Uher

1. Christ my God, my faith dis - cer - ning,
2. Mag - ni - fy, my soul, God's great - ness
3. Cal - vary's sac - ri - fice and offer - ing
4. We ad - ore the Lord our Bro - ther
Pre - sent here through heav - en's Bread,
Ev - en in the day of wrath.
In the Chal - ice and the Host -
In the Sac - ra - ment of Life
With my heart and mind a - dor - ing
Though great dark - ness falls on na - tions
Here is mer - cy like an o - cean
Cher - ish - ing his ve - ry Pres - ence
By your life my soul is fed.
Christ our Light re - veals our path.
From Our Lord in whom we boast.
Bring - ing peace to end all strife.

 copying & sharing of this music is permitted under creative commons 3.0

By your Blood my sins are cov - ered.
Let the faith - ful praise the Bo - dy
With great joy we share his Bo - dy
May we, fed by Christ's own Bo - dy,
By your grace I am re - newed.
And the Blood of Christ our Lord -
Reve - rent - ly with hearts raised up.
Serve and see God's king - dom come,
In your Spi - rit may I jour - ney
Ho - ly Wis - dom, Word e - ter - nal,
Pain or bles - sing, joy or sor - row,
And with all saints praise the Spi - rit
With your light and life im - bued.
Light and Life by all a - dored.
Lov - ing - ly we drink his Cup.
With the Fath - er and the Son.

copying & sharing of this music is permitted under creative commons 3.0 • the anthology I • www.thecatholicchoirbook.com

332

CHRIST, THE FAIR GLORY

COELITES PLAUDANT
Rabanus Maurus

1. Christ, the fair glo - ry of the ho - ly an - gels,
2. Send forth thine an - gel Mich - ael from thy pres - ence:
3. Send forth thine an - gel Gab - ri - el the migh - ty;
ru - ler of all, and au - thor of cre - a - tion,
peace - mak - er bles - sèd, may he hov - er o'er us
on strong wings fly - ing, may he come from hea - ven,
grant us in thy mer - cy grace to win by
hal - low our dwel - lings, that for us thy
drive from thy tem - ple Sa - tan the old
pa - tience realms ev - er - last - - - ing.
chil - dren all things may pros - - per.
foe - man, suc - cor our weak - ness.

 copying & sharing of this music is permitted under creative commons 3.0

4 Send forth thine angel Raphael the healer,
through him with wholesome medicines of salvation,
heal our backsliding, and in paths of goodness
guide our steps daily.

5 May the blest Mother of our God and Savior,
may all the countless company of angels,
may the assembly of the saints in glory,
ever assist us.

6 Father Almighty, Son, and Holy Spirit,
Godhead eternal, grant us our petition;
thine be the glory through the whole creation
now and for ever.

Alternate Text:

LORD OF OUR LIFE

1 Lord of our life, and God of our salvation,
Star of our night, and hope of every nation,
Hear and receive thy Church's supplication,
Lord God Almighty.

2 See round thine ark the hungry billows curling!
See how thy foes their banners are unfurling!
Lord, while their darts envenomed they are hurling,
Thou canst preserve us.

3 Lord, thou canst help when earthly armour faileth;
Lord, thou canst save when deadly sin assaileth;
Lord, o'er thy rock nor death nor hell prevaileth:
Grant us thy peace, Lord!

4 Peace, in our hearts, our evil thoughts assuaging,
Peace, in thy Church, where brothers are engaging,
Peace, when the world its busy war is waging;
Calm thy foes raging!

5 Grant us thy help till backward they are driven;
Grant them thy truth, that they may be forgiven;
Grant peace on earth, and after we have striven,
Peace in thy heaven.

Matthäus Appeles von Löwenstern

copying & sharing of this music is permitted under creative commons 3.0 • the anthology I • www.thecatholicchoirbook.com

334

COME HOLY GHOST

LAMBILOTTE 88.88 with repeat, Louis Lambilotte
Rabanus Maurus c. 800, Tr. Richard Mant, Ancient Hymns, 1837

1. Come Ho - ly Ghost, Cre - a - tor Blest, And in our
2. O Com - fort Blest to Thee we cry, Thou heav'n - ly
3. Praise be to Thee Fath - er and Son, And Ho - ly
hearts take up Thy rest; Come with Thy grace
Gift of God most high; Thou fount of life
Spi - rit Three in one; And may the Son
and heav'nl - y aid To fill the hearts which
and fire of love, And sweet a - noint - ing
on us bes - tow The gifts that from the
Thou hast made, To fill the hearts which Thou hast made.
from a - bove, And sweet a - noin - ting from a - bove.
Spi - rit flow, The gifts that from the Spi - rit flow.

 copying & sharing of this music is permitted under creative commons 3.0

COME HOLY GHOST, CREATOR COME

SOUTHWOLD

Rabanuis Maurus, Tr. Unknown

1. Come, Ho - ly Ghost, Cre - a - tor, come, From Thy bright
2. Thou who art called the Pa - ra - clete, Best gift of
3. Thou who art sev'n - fold in thy grace, Fin - ger of
heav' - nly throne: Come take pos - ses - ion of our
God a - bove, The liv - ing spring, the liv - ing
God's right hand; His pro - mise, teach - ing lit - tle
souls, And make them all your own.
fire, Sweet un - ction and true love.
ones To speak and un - der - stand.

4 O guide our minds with thy blest light,
With love our hearts inflame;
And with thy strength, which ne'er decays,
Confirm our mortal frame.

5 Far from us drive our deadly foe;
True peace unto us bring;
And through all perils lead us safe
Beneath thy sacred wing.

6 Through thee may we the Father know,
Through thee th'eternal Son,
And thee the Spirit of them both,
Thrice-blessed Three in One.

7 All glory to the Father be,
With his co-equal Son:
The same to thee, great Paraclete,
While endless ages run.

COME HOLY GHOST, WHO EVER ONE

O JESU, MI DULCISSIME

St. Ambrose of Milan, trans. Hymns Ancient & Modern, based on that of John Ellerton

1. Come Ho - ly Ghost, who ev - er one Are
2. In will and deed, by heart and tongue, With
3. Al - migh - ty Fa - ther, hear our cry Through
with the Fa - ther and the Son; Come, Ho - ly Ghost, our
all our pow'rs, your praise be sung; And love light up our
Je - sus Christ our Lord most high, Whom with the Spi - rit
souls pos - sess With your full flood of ho - li - ness.
mor - tal frame, Till oth - ers catch the liv - ing flame.
we a - dore And sing Your praise for - ev - er - more.

 copying & sharing of this music is permitted under creative commons 3.0

COME, THOU HOLY SPIRIT COME

VENI SANCTI SPIRITUS Samuel Webbe 1782
Veni Sancti Spiritus, Tr. Edwaed Caswall

1. Come Thou Ho - ly Spi - rit, come! And from Thy ce - les - tial home
2. Thou of com-for - ters the best; Thou, the soul's most wel - come Guest;
3. O most bles-sèd Light di - vine, Shine with - in these hearts of Thine,
Shed a ray of light di - vine! Come, Thou Fa - ther
Sweet re - fresh - ment here be - low; In our la - bor,
And our in - most be - ing fill! Where Thou art not,
of the poor! Come, Thou Source of all our store!
rest most sweet; Grate - ful cool - ness in the heat;
man hath naught, No - thing good in deed or thought,
Come, with - in our bos - oms shine!
So - lace in the midst of woe.
No - thing free from taint of ill.

4 Heal our wounds, our strength renew;
On our dryness pour Thy dew;
Wash the stains of guilt away;
Bend the stubborn heart and will;
Melt the frozen, warm the chill;
Guide the steps that go astray.

5 On the faithful, who adore
And confess Thee, evermore
In Thy sev'nfold gift descend;
Give them virtue's sure reward
Give them Thy salvation, Lord;
Give them joys that never end.

copying & sharing of this music is permitted under creative commons 3.0 • the anthology I • www.thecatholicchoirbook.com

CROSS OF JESUS

CROSS OF JESUS 8.7.8.7 John Stainer THE CRUCIFIXION 1887
William J. Sparrow-Simpson 1887

1. Cross of Je - sus, cross of sor - row,
2. Here the King of all the ag - es,
3. O mys - ter - ious con - des - cen - ding!
Where the blood of Christ was shed,
Throned in light ere worlds could be,
O a - ban - don - ment sub - lime!
Per - fect Per - fect Man on suf - fer,
Robed in Robed in mor - tal dy - ing,
Ve - ry Ve - ry God Him - bear - ing
Per - fect God on thee has bled!
Cru - ci - fied by sin for me.
All the suf - fer - ings of time!

 copying & sharing of this music is permitted under creative commons 3.0

339

DOWN IN ADORATION FALLING

TANTUM ERGO 8.7.8.7.8.7
St. Thomas Aquinas

1. Down in a - do - ra - tion fall - ing This great Sac - ra - ment we hail Ov - er an - cient forms of wor - ship New - er rites of grace pre - vail Faith will tell us Christ is pres - ent When our hum - an sen - ses fail.
2. To the ev - er - last - ing Fath - er And the Son who made us free And the Spir - it God pro - ceed - ing From them each e - ter - nal - ly Be sal - va - tion hon - or bless - ing Might and end - less ma - jes - ty
1. Tan - tum er - go Sa - cra - men - tum Ve - ne - re - mur cer - nu - i: Et an - ti - quum do - cu - men - tum No - vo ce - dat ri - tu - i: Prae - stet fi - des sup - ple - men - tum Sen - su - um de - fe - ctu - i. A - - - men.
2. Ge - ni - to - ri Ge - ni - to - que Laus et ju - bi - la - ti - o, - Sa - lus, ho - nor, vir - tus quo - que Sit et be - ne - dic - ti - o. Pro - ce - den - ti ab u - tro - que com - par sit lau - da - ti - o.

copying & sharing of this music is permitted under creative commons 3.0 • the anthology I • www.thecatholicchoirbook.com

FIRMLY I BELIEVE AND TRULY

DRAKES BOUGHTON 87. 87. Edward Elgar 1857-1934
Cardinal J. H. Newman

1. Firm - ly I be - lieve and tru - ly God is Three, and
2. And I trust and hope most ful - ly In that Man - hood
3. Simp - ly to His grace and wholl - y Light and life and
God is One; And I next ack - now - ledge dul - y
cru - ci - fied; And each thought and deed un - ru - ly
strength be - long, And I love sup - rem - ly sole - ly,
Man - hood ta - ken by the Son.
Do to death, as He has died.
Him the ho - ly, Him the strong.

4 And I hold in veneration,
For the love of Him alone,
Holy Church as His creation,
And her teachings are His own.

5 And I take with joy whatever
Now besets me, pain or fear,
And with a strong will I sever
All the ties which bind me here.

 copying & sharing of this music is permitted under creative commons 3.0

GLORIOUS MOTHER!

QUEEN OF HEAVEN 8.7.8.7.D
Le Jeune

1. Glor - ious Moth - er! from high hea ven Down up - on thy Chil - dren gaze,
2. Earth is dark-some, we are wear - y, Sa - tan set-teth snares for all;
3. Raise thy voice for us to Je - sus, In this bless-ed month of thine;
Gath-ered in thy own loved sea - son Thee to bless and thee to praise.
Pray for us, O ten - der Ma - ry, Pray to Je - sus lest we fall.
Raise thy pure hands up to bless us, As we lin - ger 'round thy shrine.
See, sweet Ma - ry, on thine al - tars Bloom the fair - est buds of May;
O may we, earth's sons and daugh - ters, Grow, by grace, as pure as they.

copying & sharing of this music is permitted under creative commons 3.0 • the anthology I • www.thecatholicchoirbook.com

GODHEAD HERE IN HIDING

ADORO TE DEVOTE
St. Thomas Aquinas

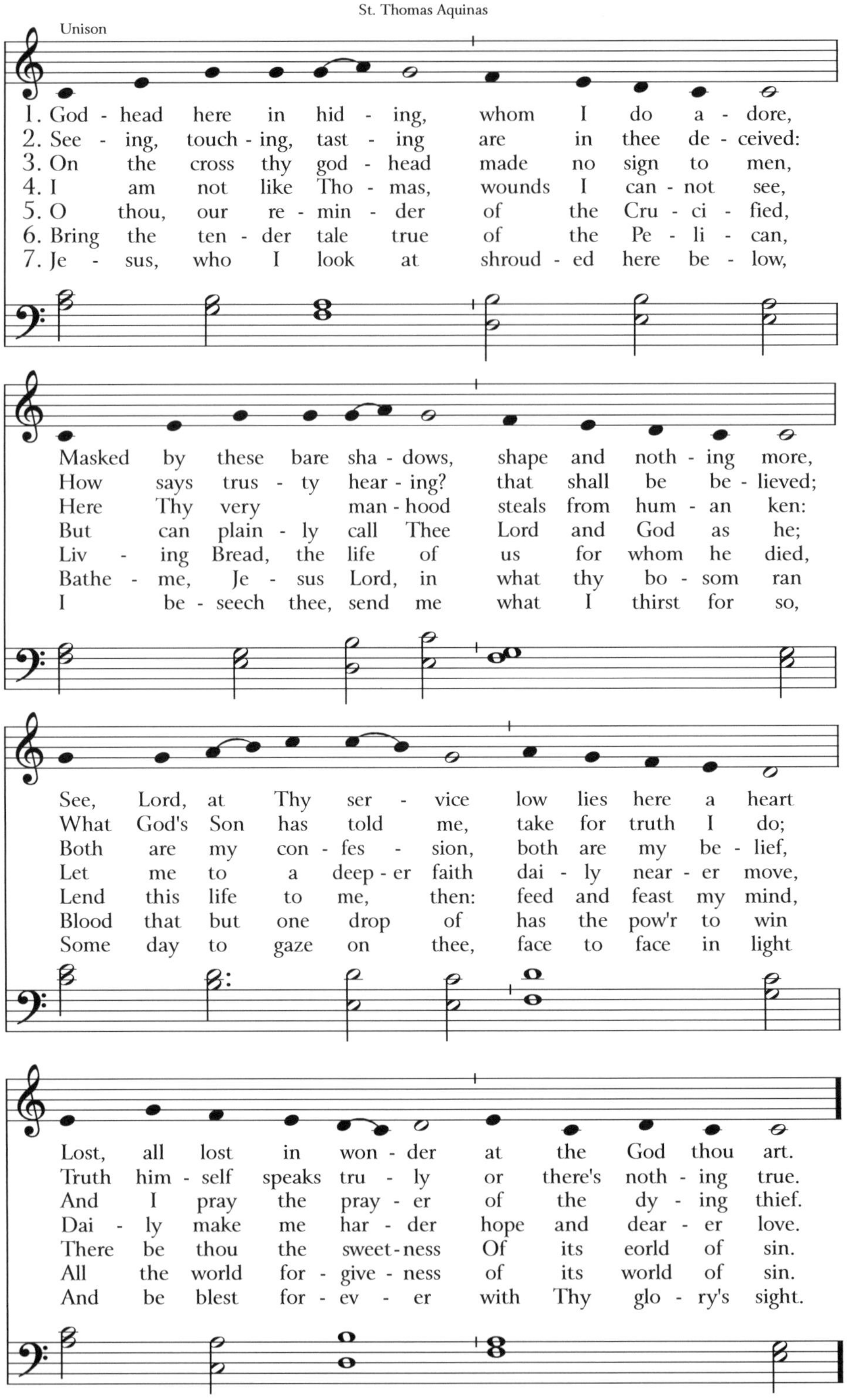
Unison
1. God - head here in hid - ing, whom I do a - dore,
2. See - ing, touch - ing, tast - ing are in thee de - ceived:
3. On the cross thy god - head made no sign to men,
4. I am not like Tho - mas, wounds I can - not see,
5. O thou, our re - min - der of the Cru - ci - fied,
6. Bring the ten - der tale true of the Pe - li - can,
7. Je - sus, who I look at shroud - ed here be - low,
Masked by these bare sha - dows, shape and noth - ing more,
How says trus - ty hear - ing? that shall be be - lieved;
Here Thy very man - hood steals from hum - an ken:
But can plain - ly call Thee Lord and God as he;
Liv - ing Bread, the life of us for whom he died,
Bathe - me, Je - sus Lord, in what thy bo - som ran
I be - seech thee, send me what I thirst for so,
See, Lord, at Thy ser - vice low lies here a heart
What God's Son has told me, take for truth I do;
Both are my con - fes - sion, both are my be - lief,
Let me to a deep - er faith dai - ly near - er move,
Lend this life to me, then: feed and feast my mind,
Blood that but one drop of has the pow'r to win
Some day to gaze on thee, face to face in light
Lost, all lost in won - der at the God thou art.
Truth him - self speaks tru - ly or there's noth - ing true.
And I pray the pray - er of the dy - ing thief.
Dai - ly make me har - der hope and dear - er love.
There be thou the sweet - ness Of its eorld of sin.
All the world for - give - ness of its world of sin.
And be blest for - ev - er with Thy glo - ry's sight.

www.thecatholicchoirbook.com • the anthology I copying & sharing of this music is permitted under creative commons 3.0

HARK! THE SOUND OF HOLY VOICES

MOULTRIE 8.7.8.7 D Gerard Francis Cobb 1838-1904
Christopher Wordsworth 1862

1. Hark! The sound of ho - ly voi-ces, chant-ing at the cry-stal sea,
2. Pa - tri - arch, and ho - ly pro-phet, who pre-pared the way of Christ
3. Mar-ching with Thy cross their ban-ner, they have tri-umphed, fol-low-ing
4. Now they reign in heav'n-ly glo - ry, now they walk in gol-den light,
Al - le - lu - ia! Al - le - lu - ia! Al - le - lu - ia! Lord, to Thee;
King, a - po - stle, saint, con-fes-sor, mar - tyr and e - van - ge - list;
Thee, the Capt-ain of sal-va-tion, Thee, their Sav-ior and their King;
Now they drink, as from a riv-er, ho - ly bliss and in - fi - nite:
Mul - ti - tude, which none can num-ber, like the stars in glo - ry stand
Saint-ly mai-den, god - ly mat-ron, wid-ows who have watched to prayer
Glad-ly, Lord, with Thee they suf-fered; gladl-y, Lord, with Thee they died;
Love and peace they taste for - ev - er, and all truth and know - ledge see
Clothed in white ap - pa - rel, hold-ing palms of vic-tory in their hand.
Joined in ho - ly con-cert, sing-ing to the Lord of all, are there.
And by death to life im-mor-tal they were born and glo - ri - fied.
In the be - a - ti - fic vis-ion of the bles-sèd Tri - ni - ty.

copying & sharing of this music is permitted under creative commons 3.0 • the anthology I • www.thecatholicchoirbook.com

JESUS, MY LORD, MY GOD, MY ALL

SWEET SACRAMENT LM with Refrain Romischkatholisches Gesangbuchlein, 1826
Fr. Frederick Faber

1. Je - sus my Lord, my God, my all.
2. Had I but Ma - ry's sin - less heart,
3. O, see, with - in a crea - ture's hand,
4. Thy bod - y, soul, and God - head, all,
5. Sound, sound His prais - es high - er still,
How can I love thee as I ought?
To love Thee with, my dear - est King;
The vast Cre - a - tor deigns to be,
O mys - ter - y of love - di - vine!
And come ye An - gels to our aid;
And how re - vere this wond - rous gift,
O with what bursts of fer - vent praise,
Re - pos - ing in - fant - like, as though
I can - not com - pass all I have,
'Tis God, 'tis God, the ve - ry God,
So far sur - pass - ing hope or thought?
Thy good - ness, Je - sus, would I sing!
On Jo - seph's arm, on Ma - ry's knee.
For all though hast and art are mine.
Whose pow'r both man and an - gels made.

www.thecatholicchoirbook.com • the anthology I copying & sharing of this music is permitted under creative commons 3.0

Sweet Sa - cra - ment, we Thee a - dore! Oh, make us
love Thee more and more. Oh, make us love Thee more and more.

copying & sharing of this music is permitted under creative commons 3.0 • the anthology I • www.thecatholicchoirbook.com

JESUS, SON OF MARY

ADORO TE DEVOTE
Edmund Stewart Palmer

Unison
1. Je - sus, Son of Mar - y, fount of life a - lone,
2. Think O Lord, in mer - cy on the souls of those
3. Of - ten were they wound - ed in the dead - ly strife;
4. Rest e - ter - nal grant them af - ter wea - ry fight;
now we hail thee pres - ent on thine al - tar throne.
who, in faith gone from us, now in death re - pose.
heal them, Good Phy - si - cian, with the balm of life.
shed on them the ra - diance of thy heaven - ly light.
Hum - bly we a - dore thee, Lord of end - less might,
Here mid stress and con - flict toils can nev - er cease;
Eve - ry taint of ev - il, frail - ty and de - cay,
Lead them on - ward, up - ward, to the ho - ly place,
in the mys - tic sym - bols veiled from earth - ly sight.
there, the warf - are end - ed, bid them rest in peace.
good and gra - cious Sav - ior, cleanse and purge a - way.
where thy saints made per - fect gaze up - on thy face.

 copying & sharing of this music is permitted under creative commons 3.0

LET ALL MORTAL FLESH

PICARDY
Liturgy of St. James

1. Let all mor - tal flesh keep si - lence, And with fear and
2. King of kings, yet born of Ma - ry, As of old on
3. Rank on rank the host of hea - ven Spreads its van-guard
4. At His feet the six winged ser - aph, Che - ru - bim with
trem - bling stand; Pon - der no - thing earth - ly
earth He stood, Lord of lords, in hu - man
on the way, As the Light of light de -
sleep - less eye, Veil their fa - ces to the
min - ded, For with bles - sing in His hand,
ves - ture, In the bo - dy and the blood;
scen - deth From the realms of end - less day,
pre - sence, As with cease - less voice they cry:

copying & sharing of this music is permitted under creative commons 3.0 • the anthology I • www.thecatholicchoirbook.com

Christ our God to earth de - scen - - - deth,
He will give to all the faith - - - ful
That the powers of hell may van - - - ish
Al - le - lu - ia, Al - le - lu - - - ia
Our full hom - age to de - mand.
His own self for heav'n - ly food.
As the dark - ness clears a - - way.
Al - le - lu - ia, Lord most high!

 copying & sharing of this music is permitted under creative commons 3.0

LIGHT'S ABODE, CELESTIAL SALEM

AD PERRENIS

Thomas à Kempis 1379-1471 Tr. John M. Neale

1. Light's a - bode, ce - les - tial Sa - lem, vi - sion
2. There for ev - er and for ev - er al - le -
3. There no cloud nor pas - sing va - por dims the
4. O how glo - rious and res - plen - dent, fra - gile
whence true peace doth spring, brigh - ter than the heart can
lu - ia is out - poured; for un - end - ing, for un -
bright - ness of the air; end - less noon - day, glo - rious
bo - dy, shalt thou be, when en - dued with heaven - ly
fan - cy, man - sion of the high - est King; O how
bro - ken is the feast - day of the Lord; all is
noon - day, from the Sun of suns is there; there no
beau - ty, full of health, and strong, and free, full of
glo - rious are the prais - es which of thee the pro - phets sing!
pure and all is ho - ly that with - in thy walls is stored.
night brings rest from la - bor, for un - known are toil and care.
vi - gor, full of plea - sure that shall last e - ter - nal - ly!

copying & sharing of this music is permitted under creative commons 3.0 • the anthology I • www.thecatholicchoirbook.com

LO! ROUND THE THRONE

ERSCHIENEN IST DER HERRLICHE TAG L.M. with Alleluai
Rowland Hill 1873

1. Lo! Round the throne, a glor - ious band, the saints in
2. Through tri - bu - lat - ion great they came; they bore the
3. They see their Sav - ior face to face, and sing the
count - less my - riads stand, of eve - ry tongue re - deemed to
cross, des - pised the shame; from all their la - bors now they
tri - umphs of his grace; him day and night they cease - less
God, ar-rayed in gar - ments washed in blood. Al - le - lu - ia!
rest, in God's e - ter - nal glo - ry blest. Al - le - lu - ia!
praise, to him the loud thanks - giv - ing raise: Al - le - lu - ia!

 copying & sharing of this music is permitted under creative commons 3.0

LORD JESUS, WHEN I THINK ON THEE

WORD OF FIRE 8.8.8.8 Noel Jones
St. Richard of Hampole d. 1349

1. Lord Je - sus, when I think of Thee, And look u - pon Thy cross a - right, Thy bo - dy stained with blood I see, Lord, pierce my heart with that sad sight!
2. Je - sus, true love I owe to Thee Who on the cross didst show, that tide, The crown of thorns, the sharp nails three, The cru - el spear that pierced Thy side.
3. Je - sus, love made Thy tears to fall, 'Twas love that made Thy blood to flow, For love wast scourged and smit - ten all, For love Thy life Thou didst fore - go.
4. Ma - ry, I pray, as thou art free, A part of this Thy grief I'll bear, That I may sor - row here with Thee, And bliss with Thee here af - ter share!

copying & sharing of this music is permitted under creative commons 3.0 • the anthology I • www.thecatholicchoirbook.com

MAIDEN MOTHER, MEEK AND MILD

ORIENTIBUS PARTIBUS 77.77.5

1. Maid - en Moth - er, meek and mild, Take, oh take me
2. Teach me, when the sun - beam bright Calls me with its
3. Teach me al - so thru the day Oft to praise my
for Thy child. All my life, oh let it be,
gol - den light, How my wak - ing thoughts may be,
heart and say, "Maid - en Moth - er meek and mild,
My best joy to think of Thee, Vir - go Ma - ri - a.
Turned to Je - sus and to thee, The Vir - gin Ma - ry.
Guard, oh, guard Thy faith - ful child!" The Vir - gin Ma - ry.

 copying & sharing of this music is permitted under creative commons 3.0

NOW MY TONGUE, THE MYSTERY TELLING

DOWLING 87.87.87 Noel Jones
PANGE LINGUA

1. Now my tongue, the mys - t'ry tell - ing, Of the glo - rious
2. That last night, at sup - per ly - ing, with the twelve,his
3. There - fore we, be - fore him bend - ing, This great Sac - ra -
4. Glo - ry let us give, and bless - ing, To the Fath - er
bod - y sing, And the blood, all price ex - cel - ling,
cho - sen band. Je - sus with the law com - ply - ing,
ment re - vere; Faith, her aid to sight is lend - ing;
and the Son. Hon - or, thanks and praise ad - dress - ing
Which the na - tions' Lord and King, Once on earth a -
keeps the feast its rites de - mand. Then, more pre - cious
Though un - seen, the Lord is near; An - cient types and
While e - ter - nal a - ges run, And the Spir - it's
mong us dwell - ing, Shed for this world's ran - som - ing.
food sup - ply - ing, Gives him - self with his own hand.
shad - ows end - ing, Christ our pas - chal Lamb is here.
pow'r con - fess - ing, Who from both with both is one.

copying & sharing of this music is permitted under creative commons 3.0 • the anthology I • www.thecatholicchoirbook.com

O BLESSED TRINITY!

Edward d'Evry
Fr. Frederick William Faber

Unison
1. O Bless-ed Tri - ni - ty! Thy chil - dren dare to lift their hearts to Thee, And bless Thy tri - ple Ma - jes - ty!
2. O Bless-ed Tr - ni - ty! Bright Son! Who art the Fa - ther's mind dis - played, Thou art be - got - ten and not made.
3. O Bless-ed Tri - ni - ty! Co - eq - ual Spi - rit! won - drous Pa - ra - clete! By Thee the God - head is com - plete.
4. O Bless-ed Tri - ni - ty! We praise Thee, bless Thee, wor - ship Thee as One, Yet Three are on the sin - gle throne.
Ho - ly Tri - ni - ty! Bles-sed E - qual Three, One God, we praise Thee.
ff

 copying & sharing of this music is permitted under creative commons 3.0

O BREAD OF HEAVEN

GILCHRIST 88.88.88.88 G. Herbert
Alphononso de' Liguori 1696-1787

1. O Bread of Heav'n! be - neath this veil,
2. O Food of Life, Thou who dost give
3. My dear - est Good! who dost so bind
Thou dost my ver - y God con - ceal. My Je - sus,
The pledge of im - mor - tal - i - ty: I live; no,
My heart with count - less chains to Thee! O sweet - est
dear - est treas - ure Hail! I love Thee and a -
'tis not I that live. God gave me life, God
Love, my soul shall find In Thy dear bonds true
dor - ing kneel. Each lov - ing soul by Thee is
lives in me. He feeds my soul, He guides my
lib - er - ty; Thy - self Thou hast be - stowed on
fed With Thine own self in form of bread.
ways, And with joy ev - 'ry grief re - pays.
me, Thine, Thine for - ev - er I will be.

copying & sharing of this music is permitted under creative commons 3.0 • the anthology I • www.thecatholicchoirbook.com

O CHRIST THE KING, THE ROYAL BANNERS RISE

GALVESTON ISLAND 10.10.10.9 Noel Jones
Vincent Uher

1. O Christ the King, the roy - al ban - ners rise.
2. Trans - fig - ured thou u - pon the moun - tain's height
3. The Cross, thy throne where thou wast lift - ed high
4. Death could not hold thee, nor a tomb con - tain,
Thy Cross, thy stan - dard we raise to the skies, And
Re - vealed the glo - ry of the Bride - groom's face And
Em - brac - ing, bro - ken and dark, the world's heart Till
O Love and Life, who from heav'n now dost reign, The
hail thee, "Lord!" and bow be - fore thine eyes.
showed to them thy pur - pose and thy Light.
blood and wa - ter gushed when pierced was Thine.
King of kings, the Lord who heal - eth pain.
Praise to Je - sus! All praise and glo - ry!

 copying & sharing of this music is permitted under creative commons 3.0

O DAY OF REST AND GLADNESS

WOODBIRD 7.6.7.6.7.6.7.6 Old German Melody
Christopher Wordsworth, 1862

1. O day of rest and glad - ness, O day of joy and light, O
2. On Thee, at the cre - a - tion, the light first had its birth; On
3. Thou art a ho - ly lad - der, where an - gels go and come; Each
4. New gra - ces ev - er gain - ing from this our day of rest, We
balm of care and sad - ness, most beau - ti - ful, most bright: On
Thee, for our sal - va - tion, Christ rose from depths of earth; On
Sun - day finds us glad - der, near - er to heaven, our home; A
reach the rest re - main - ing to spi - rits of the blessed. To
Thee, the high and low - ly, through ag - es joined in tune, Sing
Thee, our Lord, vic - to - rious, the Spi - rit sent from heaven, And
day of sweet re - fect - ion, thou art a day of love, A
Ho - ly Ghost be prai - ses, to Fath - er, and to Son; The
ho - ly, ho - ly, ho - ly, to the great God Tri - une.
thus on Thee, most glo - ri - ous, a tri - ple light was given.
day of res - ur - rec - tion from earth to things a - bove.
church her voice up - rais - es to Thee, blessed Three in One.

copying & sharing of this music is permitted under creative commons 3.0 • the anthology I • www.thecatholicchoirbook.com

O GOD UNSEEN, YET EVER NEAR

THIRD MODE MELODY C. M. D. Thomas Tallis 1505-1585
Edward Osler 1798-1863

1. O God, un-seen yet ev-er near, Thy pres-ence may we feel;
2. We come, o-be-dient to thy word, To feast on heav-'nly food;
And thus in-spired with ho-ly fear, Be-fore thine al-tar kneel.
Our meat the Bo-dy of the Lord, Our drink his pre-cious Blood.
Here may thy faith-ful peo-ple know The bless-ings of thy love,
Thus may we all thy word o-bey, For we, O God, are thine;
The streams that through the des-ert flow, The man-na from a-bove.
And go re-joic-ing on our way, Re-newed with strength di-vine.

www.thecatholicchoirbook.com • the anthology I copying & sharing of this music is permitted under creative commons 3.0

O LORD, I AM NOT WORTHY

NON DIGNUS 76.76 Traditional Melody
Landshuter Gesangbuch Tr. Unknown

1. O Lord, I am not wor - thy That
2. And hum - bly I'll re - ceive Thee, The
3. E - ter - nal Ho - ly Spi - rit, Un -
4. In - crease me faith, dear Je - sus, In
5. O Sac - ra - ment most ho - ly! O
Thou shouldst come to me, But speak the words of
Bride - groom of my soul, No more by sin to
wor - thy though I be, Pre - pare me to re -
thy rea pres - ence here. Pre - pare me to re -
Sac - ra - ment di - vine! All praise and all thanks -
com - fort, My spri - it healed shall be.
grieve Thee, Or fly Thy sweet con - trol.
ceive him, And trust the Word to me.
ceive thee, And trust the Word to me.
giv - ing, Be ev' - ry mo - ment Thine!

copying & sharing of this music is permitted under creative commons 3.0 • the anthology I • www.thecatholicchoirbook.com

O LOVE OF GOD, HOW STRONG AND TRUE

DEO GRACIAS
Horatius Bonar

1. O love of God, how strong and true!
2. O love of God, how deep and great!
3. O heav'n - ly love, how pre - cious still,
4. O love of God, our shield and stay
E - ter - nal, and yet ev - er new;
Far deep - er than man's deep - est hate;
In days of wea - ri - ness and ill,
Through all the per - ils of our way!
Un - com - pre - hen - ded and un - bought,
Self fed, self kind - led, like the light,
In nights of pain and help - less - ness,
E - ter - nal love, in thee we rest
Be - yond all know - ledge and all thought.
Change - less, e - ter - nal, in - fi - nite.
To heal, to com - fort, and to bless!
For - ev - er safe, for - ev - er blest.

 copying & sharing of this music is permitted under creative commons 3.0

O SAVING VICTIM • O SALUTARIS I

O SALUTARIS HOSTIA A. Werne
St. Thomas Aquinas

1. O sav - ing Vict - im, o - pen wide
2. To your great Name be end - less praise;
1. O sa - lu - ta - ris Ho - sti - a
2. U - ni tri - no - que Do - mi - no
The gate of Heav'n to man be - low;
Im - mor - tal God - head, One in Three;
Quae cae - li pan - dis os - ti - um.
Sit sem - pi - ter - na glo - ri - a.
Our foes press on from ev - ery side;
Grant us, for end - less length of days,
Bel - la pre - munt ho - sti - li - a,
Qui vi - tam si - ne ter - mi - no
Your aid sup - ply; Your strength be - stow.
In our true na - tive land to be.
Da ro - bur, fer aux - i - li - um.
No - bis do - net in pa - tri - a. A - men.

copying & sharing of this music is permitted under creative commons 3.0 • the anthology I • www.thecatholicchoirbook.com

O SAVING VICTIM • O SALUTARIS 2

DUGUET LM
St. Thomas Aquinas

1. O sav - ing Vict - im, o - pen wide The gate of Heav'n to
2. To your great Name be end - less praise; Im - mor - tal God - head,
1. O sa - lu - ta - ris Ho - sti - a Quae cae - li pan - dis
2. U - ni tri - no - que Do - mi - no Sit sem - pi - ter - na
man be - low; Our foes press on from ev - ery side; Your
One in Three; Grant us, for end - less length of days, In
os - ti - um. Bel - la pre - munt ho - sti - li - a, Da
glo - ri - a. Qui vi - tam si - ne ter - mi - no No -
aid sup - ply; Your strength be - stow.
our true na - tive land to be. A - - - men.
ro - bur, fer aux - i - li - um.
bis do - net in pa - tri - a. A - - - men.

Arr. Noel Jones - SAB or STB

 copying & sharing of this music is permitted under creative commons 3.0

O SPLENDOR OF GOD'S GLORY BRIGHT

PUER NOBIS NASCITUR Michael Praetorius, 1609
Ambrose of Milan, 4th Century, Tr. Robert S. Bridges

1. O splen - dor of God's glo - ry bright,
2. O thou true Sun, on us thy glance
3. The Fath - er, too, our prayers im - plore,
O thou that bring - est light from light,
let fall in roy - al ra - di - ance,
Fath - er of glo - ry ev - er - more;
O Light of Light, light's liv - ing spring,
the Spi - rit's sanc - ti - fy - ing beam
the Fath - er of all grace and might,
O Day, all days il - lu - min - ing.
up - on our earth - ly sen - ses stream.
to ban - ish sin from our de - light.

copying & sharing of this music is permitted under creative commons 3.0 • the anthology I • www.thecatholicchoirbook.com

O TRINITY OF BLESSED LIGHT

BROMLEY 8.8.8.8 Jeremiah Clarke 1700
Latin, 6th Century

1. O Tri - ni - ty of bles - sed light,
2. To thee our morn - ing song of praise,
3. All laud to God the Fa - ther be;
O U - ni - ty of prince - ly might,
to thee our even - ing pray - er we raise;
all praise, e - ter - nal Son, to thee;
the fie - ry sun now goes his way;
O grant us with thy saints on high
all glo - ry, as is ev - er meet,
shed thou with - in our hearts thy ray.
to praise thee through e - ter - ni - ty.
to God the ho - ly Pa - ra - clete.

 copying & sharing of this music is permitted under creative commons 3.0

O WHAT THEIR JOY AND GLORY MUST BE

O QUANATA QUALIA 10.10.10.10 Francois de La Feilee 1808
Peter Abelard

1. O what their joy and their glo - ry must be,
2. Tru - ly, "Je - ru - sa - lem" name we that shore,
3. There, where no trou - bles dis - trac - tion can bring,
4. Now, in the mean - time, with hearts raised on high,
5. Low be - fore him with our prais - es we fall,
those end - less Sab - baths the bles - sèd ones see;
ci - ty of peace that brings joy ev - er - more;
we the sweet an - thems of Zi - on shall sing;
we for that coun - try must yearn and must sigh,
of whom and in whom and through whom are all;
crown for the val - iant, to wear - y ones rest:
wish and ful - fill - ment are not sev - ered there,
while for thy grace, Lord, their voi - ces of praise
seek - ing Je - ru - sa - lem, dear na - tive land,
of whom, the Fath - er; and in whom, the Son;
God shall be All, and in all ev - er blest.
nor do things prayed for come short of the prayer, -
thy bles - sèd peo - ple e - ter - nal - ly raise.
through our long ex - ile on Ba - by-lon's strand.
through whom, the Spi - rit, with them ev - er One.

copying & sharing of this music is permitted under creative commons 3.0 • the anthology I • www.thecatholicchoirbook.com

O WHERE ARE KINGS AND EMPIRES NOW

RODMELL 8.7.8.7
A. Cleveland Coxe 1818-1896

Unison
1. O where are kings and em - pires now Of
2. We mark her good - ly bat - tle - ments, And
3. For not like king - doms of the world, Thy
4. Un - shak - en as e - ter - nal hills, Im -
old that went and came But, Lord, thy Church is
her foun - da - tions strong: We hear with - in the
ho - ly Church, O God: Tho' earth - quake shocks are
mo - va - ble she stands, A moun - tain that shall
pray - ing yet, Two thou - sand years the same.
sol - emn voice Of her un - end - ing song.
threat'n - ing her, And tem - pests are a - broad;
fill the earth, A house not made by hands.

 copying & sharing of this music is permitted under creative commons 3.0

ONLY-BEGOTTEN, WORD OF GOD ETERNAL

ROUEN 87.87.87 Old French Church Melody
9th Century, Tr. Maxwell Julius Blacker 1884

Unison
1. On - ly - Be - got - ten, Word of God e - ter - nal,
2. This is thy tem - ple; here thy pres - ence - cham - ber;
3. Here in our sick - ness heal - ing grace a - boun - deth,
4. Hal - lowed this dwel - ling where the Lord a - bi - deth,
5. God in three Per - sons, Fath - er ev - er - last - ing,
Lord of Cre - a - tion, mer - ci - ful and migh - ty,
Here may thy ser - vants, at the mys - tic ban - quet,
Light in our blind - ness, in our toil re - fresh - ment;
This is none oth - er than the gate of Hea - ven;
Son co - e - ter - nal, ev - er bles - sèd Spi - rit,
List to thy ser - vants, when their tune - ful
Hum - bly a - dor - ing, take thy Bo - dy
Sin is for - gi - ven, hope o'er fear pre -
Stran - gers and pil - grims, mak - ing homes e -
Thine be the glo - ry, praise and a - do -
voi - ces Rise to thy pres - - - - ence.
bro - ken, Drink of thy chal - - - - ice.
vail - eth, Joy o - ver sor - - - - row.
ter - nal, Pass through its por - - - - tals.
ra - tion, Now and for - ev - - - - er.

copying & sharing of this music is permitted under creative commons 3.0 • the anthology I • www.thecatholicchoirbook.com

REJOICE IN THE LORD

CAMPBELL LANE 1010.11.11 Noel Jones
Vincent Uher

1. Re - joice in the Lord, O friends of God's Son. The
2. How gra - cious is God, how migh - ty and just. His
3. The Spirit and Bride bid all of us come. The
feast is pre - pared, the wai - ting is done. The
mer - cies are sure and wor - thy of trust. Come,
thirs - ty shall drink from our Fa - ther's love. The
ban - quet is spread with warm wel - come for all. O
bro - ken and wea - ry. Come, bur - dened and torn. With
hun - gry shall feed on the joys of the Lord, And
do not de - lay, but re - spond to God's call!
crowns of sal - va - tion Christ shall you a - dorn.
Jes - us the Christ will be e - ver a - dored.

 copying & sharing of this music is permitted under creative commons 3.0

ROUND THE LORD, IN GLORY SEATED

RUSTINGTON
Richard Mant

1. Round the Lord in glo - ry sea - ted, che - ru - bim and se - ra - phim
2. Heav'n is still with glo - ry ring - ing, earth takes up the an - gels' cry,
3. "Lord, thy glo - ry fills the hea - ven, earth is with its ful - ness stored;
filled his temp - le, and re - pea - ted each to each the_al - ter - nate
"Ho - ly, ho - ly, ho - ly," sing - ing, "Lord of Hosts, the Lord most
un - to thee be glo - ry gi - ven, ho - ly, ho - ly, ho - ly
hymn: "Lord, thy glo - ry fills the hea - ven, earth is
high." With his se - raph train be - fore Him, with his
Lord!" Thus thy glo - rious Name con - fes - sing, we a -
with its ful - ness stored; un - to thee be glo - ry
ho - ly church be - low, thus con - spire we to a -
dopt thine an - gels' cry, "Ho - ly, ho - ly, ho - ly,"
gi - ven, ho - ly, ho - ly, ho - ly Lord!"
dore him, bid we thus our an - them flow.
bles - sing thee, the Lord of Hosts most high.

copying & sharing of this music is permitted under creative commons 3.0 • the anthology I • www.thecatholicchoirbook.com

370

SEE, AMID THE WINTER'S SNOW

HUMILITY 77.77 WITH REFRAIN John Goss 1871 Descant Noel Jones
Edward Caswell 1858

Unison
1. See a - mid the win - ter's snow,
2. Lo, with - in a man - ger lies
3. "As we watched at dead of night,
4. O teach us, Ho - ly Child, By
Born for us on Earth be - low,
He who built the star - ry skies;
Lo, we saw a wond - rous light:
Thy face so meek and mild, Teach
See, the ten - der Lamb ap - pears,
He who, throned in height sub - lime,
An - gels sing - ing 'Peace On Earth'
us to re - sem - ble Thee, In

www.thecatholicchoirbook.com • the anthology I copying & sharing of this music is permitted under creative commons 3.0

Prom - ised from e - ter - nal years.
Sits a - mong the cher - u - bim.
Told us of the Sav - iour's birth."
Thy sweet hu - mi - li - ty. O
Last Verse Descant
[Parts] Hail that ev - er bles - sèd morn, hail re-demp - tion's
hap - py dawn, sing through all Je - ru - sa-lem:
Christ is born in Beth - le - hem.

SING, MY SOUL, HIS WONDROUS LOVE

ST. BEES 7.7.7.7 John Bacchus Dykes 1862
Anonymous 1800

1. Sing, my soul, his wondrous love,
2. Heaven and earth by him were made;
3. God, the mer - ci - ful and good,
4. Sing, my soul, a - dore his Name!
who from yon bright throne a - bove,
all is by his scep - ter swayed;
bought us with the Sav - ior's blood,
Let his glo - ry be thy theme:
ev - er watch - ful o'er our race,
what are we that he should show
and, to make our safe - ty sure,
praise him till he calls thee home;
still to us ex - tends his grace.
so much love to us bel - ow?
guides us by his Spi - rit pure.
truth his love for all to come.

www.thecatholicchoirbook.com • the anthology I copying & sharing of this music is permitted under creative commons 3.0

VIRGIN-BORN, WE KNEEL BEFORE THEE

HARRIET 8.8.7.7.
Reginald Heber 1783-1826

1. Vir - gin - born, we kneel be - fore Thee;
2. Bless - ed was the breast that fed Thee;
3. Bless - ed she by all cre - a - tion,
Bless - ed was the womb that bore Thee;
Bless - ed was the hand that led Thee;
Who brought forth the world's sal - va - tion,
Ma - ry, Moth - er meek and mild,
Bless - ed was the watch she kept
Bless - ed they, for - ev - er blest,
Bless - ed was she in her Child.
As the Ho - ly Christ Child slept.
Who love most and serve Thee best.

copying & sharing of this music is permitted under creative commons 3.0 • the anthology I • www.thecatholicchoirbook.com

WHO ARE THESE LIKE STARS APPEARING

ALL SAINTS 8.7.8.7.7.7 Geistreiches Gesangbuch, Darmstadt, 1698
Heinrich Theobald Schenk 1719 Tr. Francis Elizabeth Cox

1. Who are these like stars ap - pear - ing, these, be - fore God's
2. Who are these of dazz - ling bright - ness, clothed in God's own
3. These are they who have con - ten - ded for their Sav - ior's
throne who stand? Each a gol - den crown is wear - ing;
righ - teous - ness These, in robes of pur - est white - ness,
hon - or long, wrestl - ing on till life was end - ed,
who are all this glo - rious band? Al - le - lu - ia!
shall their lus - ter still pos - sess, still un - touched by
fol - l'wing not the sin - ful - throng. these who well the
Hark, they sing, prais - ing loud their heaven - ly King.
time's rude hand? Whence came all this glor - ious band?
fight sus - tained, tri - umph through the Lamb have gained.

www.thecatholicchoirbook.com • the anthology I copying & sharing of this music is permitted under creative commons 3.0

WORD OF GOD TO EARTH DESCENDING

DRAKES BOUGHTON 87. 87. Edward Elgar 1857-1934
Thomas Aquinas Tr. Robert Campbell 1833-1868

1. Word of God to earth de - scend - ing, with the Fa - ther
2. Well the trait - or's kiss fore - know - ing, Mir - a - cle of
3. Might - y Vic - tim, earth's sal - va - tion, Heav'n - ly gates un -
4. Ho - ly bo - dy, blood all pre - cious, Giv'n by him to
pres - ent still, Near His earth - ly jour - ney's end - ing
love di - vine, See His hands him - self be - stow - ing
fold - ing wide, Help thy peo - ple in temp - ta - tion,
be our food, With them both he doth re - fresh us,
Hastes His mis - sion to ful - fill.
In the hal - lowed Bread and Wine.
Feed them from Thy bleed - ing side.
Formed like him of flesh and blood.

5 Mighty Victim, earth's salvation,
Heaven's own gate unfolding wide,
Help thy people in temptation,
Feed them from thy bleeding side.

6 Unto thee, the hidden manna,
Father, Spirit, unto thee,
Let us raise the loud hosanna,
And adoring bend the knee.

copying & sharing of this music is permitted under creative commons 3.0 • the anthology I • www.thecatholicchoirbook.com

58. CRUX FIDELIS, Hymn for Good Friday

I
CRux fi-dé-lis, inter omnes Arbor una nó-bi- lis:
Nulla silva ta-lem pro-fert, Fronde, flo- re, gérmi- ne:
* Dulce lignum, dulces clavos, Dulce pondus sústi-net.

O faithful Cross, incomparable Tree, the noblest of all; no forest hath ere put forth the likes of thine own leaves, thy flowers, thy fruits;

* Gentle wood with a gentle nail, to support so gentle a burden!

1. Pange, lingua, gloriósi
Láuream certáminis,
Et super crucis trophǽo
Dic triumphum nóbilem:
Quáliter Redémptor orbis
Immolátus vícerit.
Crux...gérmine.

1. Sing, O my tongue, of the battle, of the glorious struggle; and over the trophy of the Cross, proclaim the noble triumph; tell how the Redeemer of the world won victory through his sacrifice.

2. De paréntis protoplásti
Fraude Factor cóndolens,
Quando pomi noxiális
In necem morsu ruit:
Ipse lignum tunc notávit,
Damna lign*i* ut sólveret.
** Dulce.*

2. The Creator looked on sadly as the first man, our forefather, was deceived, and as he fell into the snare of death, taking a bite of a lethal fruit; it was then that God chose this blessed piece of wood to destroy the other tree's curse.

3. Hoc opus nostræ salútis
Ordo depopóscerat:
Multifórmis proditóris
Ars ut artem fálleret:
Et medélam ferret inde,
Hostis unde lǽserat.

Crux...gérmine.

3. Such was the act called for by the economy of our salvation: to outwit the resourceful craftiness of the Traitor and to obtain our remedy from the very weapon with which our enemy struck.

www.thecatholicchoirbook.com • the anthology | copying & sharing of this music is permitted under creative commons 3.0

4. Quando venit ergo sacri
Plenitúdo témporis,
Missus est ab arce Patris
Natus, orbis Cónditor,
Atque ventre virgináli
Carn*e* amíctus pródiit.
* *Dulce.*

4. And so, when the fullness of that blessed time had come, the Son, the Creator of the world, was sent from the throne of the Father, and having become flesh, he came forth from the womb of a virgin.

5. Vagit infans inter arcta
Cónditus præsépia:
Membra pannis involúta
Virgo Mater álligat:
Et Dei manus pedésque
Stricta cingit fáscia.
Crux...gérmine.

5. The infant cried as he was placed in the narrow manger; his Virgin Mother wrapped his limbs in swaddling clothes, encircling God's hands and feet with tight bands.

6. Lustra sex qui jam perégit,
Tempus implens córporis,
Sponte líbera Redémptor
Passióni déditus,
Agnus in Crucis levátur
Immolándus stípite.
* *Dulce.*

6. When more than thirty years had past, at the end of his earthly life, he willingly gave himself up to the Passion; it was for this that he was born. The Lamb was lifted up onto a Cross, offered in sacrifice on wood.

7. Felle potus ecce languet:
Spina, clavi, láncea,
Mite corpus perforárunt,
Unda manat et cruor:
Terra, pontus, astra, mundus,
Quo lavántur flúmine!
Crux...gérmine.

7. Behold the vinegar, the gall, the reed, the spittle, the nails and spear! His precious body is torn open, water and blood rush forth. This great and mighty river washes land, sea, stars—the entire world!

8. Flecte ramos, arbor alta,
Tensa laxa víscera,
Et rigor lentéscat ille,
Quem dedit natívitas:
Et supérni membra Regis
Tende miti stípite.
* *Dulce.*

8. Bend thy branches, tallest of trees, relax thy hold on his tightly stretched body; soften up the hardness which nature hath given thee, and present to the body of the Heavenly King a more bearable support.

copying & sharing of this music is permitted under creative commons 3.0 • the anthology I • www.thecatholicchoirbook.com

4. Ave verum Corpus, *in Honor of the Blessed Sacrament*

VI
A - ve ve-rum Corpus na-tum de Ma-rí- a Vírgi-ne:
Ve- re passum, immo-lá-tum in cruce pro hómi-ne: Cu-jus
la-tus perfo-rá- tum flu-xit aqua et sángui-ne: Esto
no-bis prægustá- tum mortis in ex-ámi-ne. O Je- su
dul- cis! O Je- su pi- e! O Je- su fi-li Ma-rí- æ.

Hail, true Body, born of Mary the Virgin; truly suffering, sacrificed on the cross for man; from Whose pierced side flowed water and blood. Be to us a foretaste at death's trial, O sweet Jesus, O loving Jesus, O Jesus Son of Mary.

 copying & sharing of this music is permitted under creative commons 3.0

10. *JESU DULCIS MEMORIA, in Honor of the Name of Jesus*

I

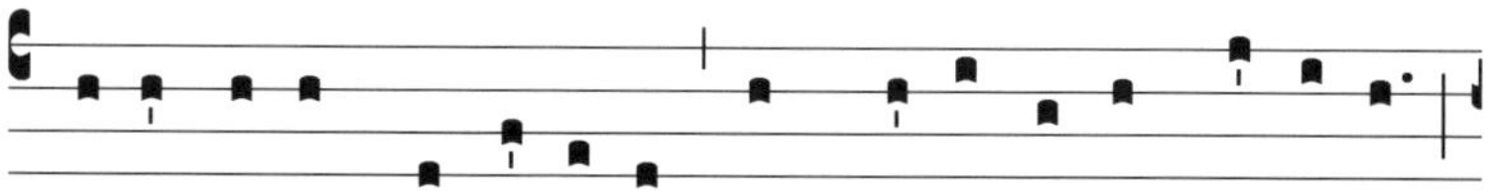

JEsu dulcis memó-ri- a, Dans ve-ra cordis gáudi- a:

Sed super mel et ómni- a, E-jus dulcis præ-sénti- a.

How sweet the memory of Jesus, giving joy to true hearts; but beyond honey and all else, is the sweetness of His presence.

2. Nil cánitur suávius,
Nil audítur jucúndius,
Nil cogitátur dúlcius,
Quam Jesus Dei Fílius.

2. Nothing is sung more sweetly, nothing heard with more delight, nothing thought more dear, than Jesus, God's Son.

3. Jesu spes pæniténtibus,
Quam pius es peténtibus!
Quam bonus te quæréntibus!
Sed quid inveniéntibus?

3. Jesus, hope of penitents, how kind to those who beg, how good to those who seek: but what art Thou to those who find Thee!

4. Nec lingua valet dícere,
Nec líttera exprímere:
Expértus potest crédere,
Quid sit Jesum dilígere.

4. Tongue cannot speak, pen cannot write; experience alone can believe, what it is to love Jesus.

5. Sis Jesu nostrum gáudium,
Qui es futúrus præmium:
Sit nostra in te glória,
Per cuncta semper sǽcula.

5. Be thou, O Jesus, our joy, Who shall be our reward: in Thee, may there be for us great glory, through everlasting ages.

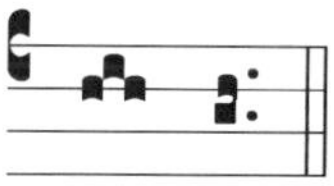

A- men.

℣. Sit nomen Dómini benedíctum.
℟. Ex hoc nunc, et usque in sǽculum.

℣. May the Name of the Lord be blessed. ℟. Both now, and for ever.

copying & sharing of this music is permitted under creative commons 3.0 • the anthology I • www.thecatholicchoirbook.com

51. STABAT MATER, at the Stations of the Cross

VI
S Ta-bat Ma-ter do-lo- ró-sa Juxta cru-cem lacri-
mó-sa, Dum pendé-bat Fí- li- us.

Sorrowful, weeping stood the Mother by the cross on which hung her Son.

2. Cujus ánimam geméntem,
Contristátam et doléntem
Pertransívit gládius.

2. Whose soul, mournful, sad, lamenting, was pierced by a sword.

3. O quam tristis et afflícta
Fuit illa benedícta
Mater Unigéniti!

3. Oh how sad, how afflicted was that blessed Mother of the Only-begotten.

4. Quæ mærébat et dolébat,
Pia Mater, dum vidébat
Nati pœnas ínclyti.

4. How did she mourn and lament, loving Mother, while she saw the torment of her divine Son.

5. Quis est homo qui non fleret,
Matrem Christi si vidéret
In tanto supplício?

5. What man would not weep if he saw the mother of Christ in such sorrow?

6. Quis non posset contristári,
Christi matrem contemplári
Doléntem cum Fílio?

6. Who would not mourn with her, seeing Christ's mother mourning with her Son?

7. Pro peccátis suæ gentis,
Vidit Jesum in torméntis,
Et flagéllis súbditum.

7. For the sins of his race she sees Jesus scourged and in torment.

8. Vidit suum dulcem natum
Moriéndo desolátum,
Dum emísit spíritum.

8. She sees her dear Son dying in anguish, as he gives up the ghost.

9. Eia Mater, fons amóris,
Me sentíre vim dolóris
Fac, ut tecum lúgeam.

9. O Mother, fount of love, make me feel the strength of thy sorrow, that I may mourn with thee.

www.thecatholicchoirbook.com • the anthology I copying & sharing of this music is permitted under creative commons 3.0

10. Fac ut árdeat cor meum
In amándo Christum Deum,
Ut sibi compláceam.

10. Make my heart burn with love for Christ my God, that I may please him.

11. Sancta Mater, istud agas,
Crucifíxi fige plagas
Cordi meo válide.

11. Holy Mother, do this: fix the wounds of the Crucified firmly in my heart.

12. Tui nati vulneráti,
Tam dignáti pro me pati,
Pœnas mecum dívide.

12. Share with me the pain of thy wounded Son, Who deigns to bear so much for me.

13. Fac me tecum pie flere,
Crucifíxo condolére,
Donec ego víxero.

13. While I live let me mourn with thee, suffering with Him Who bore the cross.

14. Juxta crucem tecum stare,
Et me tibi sociáre
In planctu desídero.

14. I wish to stand with thee by the cross and to share thy woe.

15. Virgo vírginum præclára,
Mihi jam non sis amára:
Fac me tecum plángere.

15. Blessed Virgin of all virgins, be not hard to me, let me weep with thee.

16. Fac ut portem Christi mortem,
Passiónis fac consórtem,
Et plagas recólere.

16. Let me remember the death of Christ, give me a share in his passion, thinking of his pain.

17. Fac me plagis vulnerári,
Fac me cruc*e* inebriári,
Et cruóre Fílii.

17. Let me be wounded with his wounds, be filled with the cross and precious blood of thy Son.

18. Flammis ne urar succénsus,
Per te, Virgo, sim defénsus
In die judícii.

18. That I may not burn in flames, may I be protected by thee, holy Virgin, at the day of judgment.

19. Christe, cum sit hinc exíre,
Da per Matrem me veníre
Ad palmam victóriæ.

19. Christ, when I come to death, grant that through Thy Mother, I may gain the palm of victory.

20. Quando corpus moriétur,
Fac ut ánimæ donétur
Paradísi glória.

20. When the body dies, grant that my soul may enter the glory of paradise.

copying & sharing of this music is permitted under creative commons 3.0 • the anthology I • www.thecatholicchoirbook.com

Hymn before Benediction

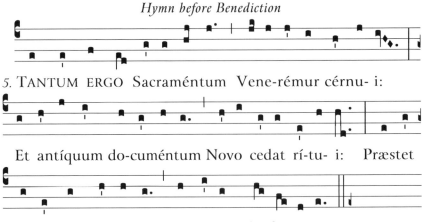

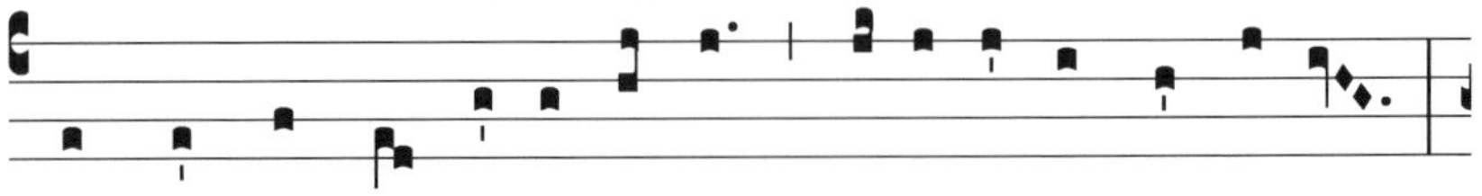

5. TANTUM ERGO Sacraméntum Vene-rémur cérnu- i:

Et antíquum do-cuméntum Novo cedat rí-tu- i: Præstet

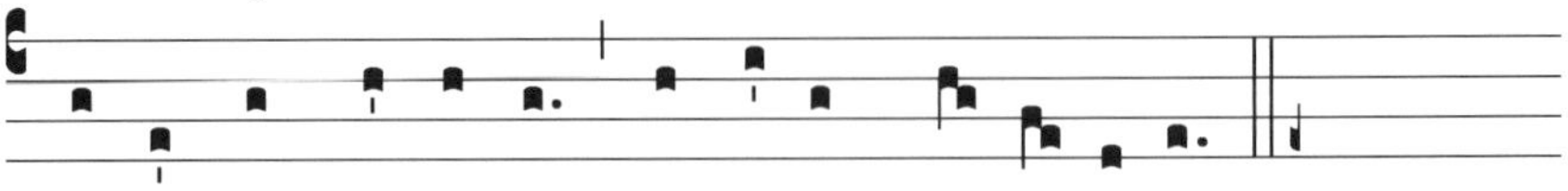

fi-des suppleméntum Sensu- um de- féctu- i.

Bowing low then let us worship so great a Sacrament. The old law gives place to a new rite, faith supplies the lack of sight.

6. Genitóri, Genitóque
Laus et jubilátio,
Salus, honor, virtus quoque
Sit et benedíctio:
Procedénti ab utróque
Compar sit laudátio.

6. To the Father and to the Son be praise and glory, salvation, honor, power and blessing; to Him Who from both proceeds be the same worship.

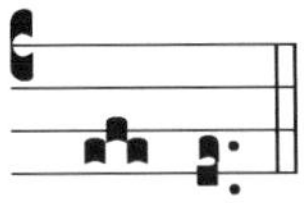

A-men.

30. AVE MARIA

I

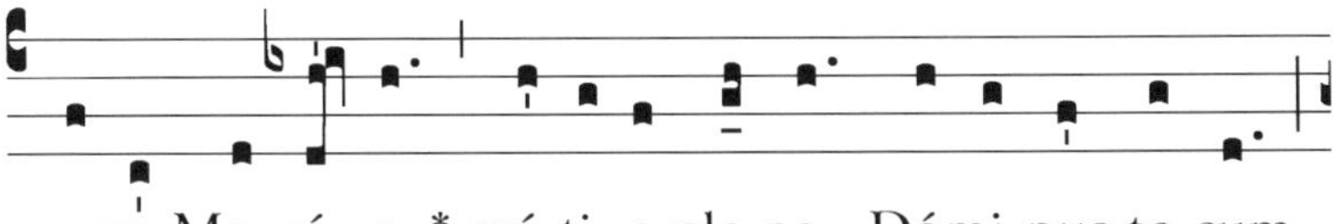

A - ve Ma- rí- a, * grá-ti- a ple-na, Dómi-nus te-cum,

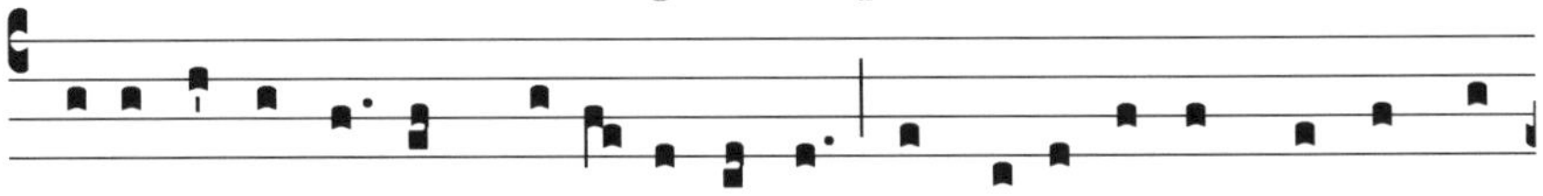

bene-dícta tu in mu-li- é- ri-bus, et bene-díctus fructus ven-

tris tu- i, Je-sus. Sancta Ma-rí- a, Ma-ter De- i, o-ra pro

nobis pecca- tó-ribus, nunc et in ho- ra mortis nostræ. Amen.

Hail Mary, full of grace! the Lord is with thee; blessed art thou among women, and blessed is the fruit of thy womb, Jesus. Holy Mary, Mother of God, pray for us sinners, now and at the hour of our death. Amen.

 copying & sharing of this music is permitted under creative commons 3.0

Pages from *The Parish Book of Chant*
are reprinted here with permission of
The Church Music Association of America.

WWW.MUSICASACRA.COM

THE PULSE OF MUSIC

Book 1
A Beginner's Guide To Reading Gregorian Chant Notation
Book 2
A Beginner's Guide To Singing Gregorian Chant Rhythm and Solfeggio
Books 1 & 2 Combined
A Beginner's Guide to Singing Gregorian Chant Notation, Rhythm and Solfeggio

A Gregorian Chant Coloring Book for Children & Adults
Student Edition • Teacher's Edition

If you can sing "Joy to the World" you can learn to read and sing Gregorian Chant
For people who can and cannot read music.

Gregorian Chant Blank Staff Notebook

The Catholic Choirbook Series
Volumes 1 - 5
www.thecatholicchoirbook.com

The Catholic Choirbook Anthology I
&
The Catholic Choirbook Choir Training Guide

The Catholic Hymnal

www.thecatholichymnal.com

Noel Jones, AAGO • Creative Director
Ellen Doll Jones, CAGO • Editor

Frog Music Press

201 County Road 432 --- Englewood, TN 37329 --- 423 887-7594

Made in the USA
Middletown, DE
19 September 2024

60681976R00239